LAUREL LEE'S
JOURNAL

LAUREL LEE'S
JOURNAL

combining WALKING THROUGH THE FIRE
and SIGNS OF SPRING

CHRISTIAN HERALD BOOKS
Chappaqua, New York 10514

First combined edition: 1980 Laurel Lee's Journal

Library of Congress
Catalog Card Number: 80-66574
ISBN: 0-915684-75-6

Christian Herald Books
40 Overlook Drive
Chappaqua, New York 10514

Printed in the United States of America

To my father, James Moore,
                    and my mother, Ruth Moore;

    "Honor thy father and mother,
    that thy days may be long upon the land."

And to my brothers and sisters who have been,
                    and will be.

When thou walkest through the fire,
thou shall not be burned,
neither shall the flame be kindled upon thee.

Isaiah 43:2

In my palm was a handful of cards.
"Look doctor," I said, "let's read
them together." The favored one
read "pregnant" while the others
said "anemia" and "cough." I didn't
know what a long game it was going
to be and just how stacked was the deck . . .

The family practice clinic is located in a separate building within the multiservice cluster of the University of Oregon Medical School. One physician cares for the medical problems of the entire family unit. For my prenatal care, I was assigned to Dr. Michael Mainer, who was in his third year of residency.

Once a month I would ride the bus to Emma Jones Hall at the top of the hill. Once a month Dr. Mainer would record the early prenatal questions and answers.

He was a number genius. My weight was the first data of his inquiry. He could remember my previous scores without the chart, as if he were a collector of fat-lady baseball cards.

He chided me the month I splurged on peanut butter cookies.

"Oh, it's my hiking boots," I said, clicking my heels together.

"Well, maybe," he answered.

After each visit the children and I would eat a picnic in the forest behind the building, and once we built a fort.

Sometimes medical students also would bring their lunch bags into the sunshine. I would listen to their conversation. All they seemed to talk about was who among their classmates and teaching staff smoked cigarettes.

I did not know if I were young and they were old or if I were old and they were young.

Also in the world at this time was a man who made certain powerful additions to his motorcycle and with a parachute and a great deal of publicity intended to jump the Snake River Canyon. He crashed, but lived. The same week I had my own cycle adventure. My son balanced on my bicycle crossbar. It was the most expedient way to go to the grocery store. What I gained in speed was a haste that made waste. It was a study of gravity. The bike went down the hill. Matthew's boot gravitated to the spokes. The obstruction abruptly halted all speed. Matthew jumped and escaped our collapse, but the accident caused my knee to swell. I went to the doctor and had my first X ray and rode in my first wheelchair. My knee was fine but I was miserable that my bike was broken.

Every night I experienced a phenomenon that I regarded as a mystery of my pregnancy. As soon as I slept I would perspire until the discomfort of my wet nightclothes would wake me. My body could produce such an abundance of water in the night sweat I thought I was turning into a mermaid, but could not complete the chemistry.

> There was a cold.
> In the middle of the cold
> There was a cough.
> It never went away,
> But came to stay.

the night was
a long passage
to light.

The cough always wanted to be heard:
"I will not cough," I said, and counted
as long as I could. The COUGH won.
"I will hold my breath," I said.
But the COUGH won.
"I will suck green cough-killer drops," I said.
But the COUGH won again.

Friday—October 3, 1975

When the cough coughed all night I went up on the hill again. Dr. Mainer pulled up on his bicycle just as I arrived at the door. "I'm sick," I said, and he told me to get a chest X ray.

"No. I'm pregnant and X rays aren't good. Anyway, I don't smoke cigarettes and nothing is that serious."

He listened, but did not waver. He said, "I'm going that way," and walked me to the X-ray department. He told me to bring my X rays back to the clinic. We stepped into an elevator and Dr. Mainer introduced me to Dr. Stu Levy, who operated the elevator buttons as if we were all in a department store, calling out the merchandise on each floor:

"PHOTOGRAPHIC EQUIPMENT,
PHOTOGRAPHY
NUMBER 3"

I walked out with Matthew and Anna following me like puppies. The technicians shielded me with a lead apron over a white gown. When I was dressed, they asked to do another view and they wouldn't let me take my X rays to the family practice office. I was heavy inside, as if I were still wearing their shield. Even the air felt dense in the waiting room.

The kingdom of my two children tap-danced through the day. Wonder lay at their every corner:

Imagine seeing a machine that takes pictures of the inside of bodies.

Imagine seeing real pictures of real bones on real lighted screens.

They lay on the floor and watched the old Otis elevator with all its cables go up and down.

I was called to the examining room and sat under one of the bright posters that bright doctors' offices always seem to have.

"What does the sign say, Mother?"

"Oh, that is true!" (Matthew, age 5).

The doctors' faces were a professional grim. The one with Dr. Mainer was from surgery, a doctor I never saw again. He indicated to me my very own bone poster, with an extra white sac hanging next to the lung. He brought in those first enrollment papers of my family's medical history and asked about the notation of cancer on my mother's side.

He asked how many children I had, and indicated a real concern about my pregnancy, now starting its sixth month. As they examined me the doctors exchanged, with their eyes, their verification of swollen lymph nodes in my neck. They talked their serious talk in the hall, and I could hear them when my childrens' chattering permitted me. I could hear the word *tumor*.

I was full of plans for the future, like a tree of leaves. They fell off the branches at once, not blowing away, but laid at the root.

I was in myself, receiving a new dimension of concerns, and I was outside myself, watching myself receive it. I was not upset, and I puzzled at this:

> When it rains all winter and our house shrinks to where my outstretched arms can touch the walls; I run outside and shout at the hedge "HOW MANY PEOPLE CAN WE FIT IN A PHONE BOOTH?"
> When the children both cry at once, demand at once, fight at once, and break at once; then the violin strings in my mind snap, and I have no melody.
> When Richard walks through the house, his head turning into a growling bear, I faint away inside.

I called Richard from the hall phone, outlining the events of the day and the pending hospitalization the following Monday.

I walked outside thinking, "I get to think about things that usually would be held from me until later seasons of life. Wisdom is the principal thing." My body rode the bus home, and I executed the correct mechanical procedures to transport us, but my mind kept sorting images.

My experience that Friday encompassed six hours at the doctor's office. That night I had a strange dream: A photographer had come to take yearbook pictures at the clinic, and all the staff formed in lines on the steps of Emma Jones Hall—lines of doctors smiling. Then someone said, "She's been here so long, include her in the shot." Thus, we were all recorded in black and white.

Saturday—October 4, 1975

The doctors were too serious for me not to be serious. I made an appointment within myself to consider dying. I wanted to look in the face of death, sit on its lap and smell its breath.

I had seen life as an ongoing stream that I was just immersed in. I always felt that its path would take me to the outermost parts of the earth. Portland was only a temporary camping spot for the nurture of young children. In one stroke I cut with some mental shears that fifty-more-year river, leaving me a short stretch.

I cried. I wept sore. I wanted the privilege of guiding the arrows of my children and giving them the wisdom that could shoot them into the high place.

I was melancholy. My memory pulled out special days and old ways that had had their fragrance.

Even the meditation of death progresses. It was like a dark glass I had to pass through. Death is the last enemy.

Music came. Chorus and voices, in tones and scales, in patterns and textures, repeating a joyous sound.

I was free. I felt I could fly around the room. I knew it would all have to be faced again; some more black-and-white runs, and once in living color.

HOSPITAL
OCT. 6

I had never really been in a hospital before, except to walk in and out with a new baby.

After being admitted and issued a plastic bag of necessities (including toilet paper), I was delivered to a bed.

There was a voice in the ceiling out in the hall that spent its days and nights calling doctors' names.

I landed in another planet, and suffered from some manifestation of cultural shock.

THE VITAL SIGN SONG

"It's best to rest but NURSES made tests. It went on graphs for the doctor, staff."

My first morning found a group of family practice doctors clustered by my bed. Dr. Mainer made his introductory remark: "This patient weighs one hundred and sixty pounds."

I felt instantly reduced to a county fair 4-H Club entry. I was not silent as a sheep before my shearers, but with a touch of sarcasm repeated: "Yes, this patient weighs one hundred and sixty pounds." Then I was so embarrassed; I wanted them to just go away. One by one they felt my swollen lymph nodes. Then they left to complete their rounds.

When I was first introduced to my chest X ray, the doctor had said, "This presents certain ethical considerations in regard to the pregnancy." From that time

I knew the baby was threatened. It was ironic that my first roommate had come for an abortion, although she was equally advanced in her pregnancy.

At an appointed hour, the yellow curtains were drawn around her bed, and she was given an abdominal saline injection. I felt anguish.

I had my own recreations. Two doctors, aided by a nurse, came to get a sample of bone marrow. I studiously avoided their tray of tools. I lay on my stomach and bit my pillow. It hurt very much, and it seemed to go on for a long time. So I pretended it was the days of the Inquisition. I was being tortured for Truth, and I would not accept deliverance. Later, their excavation site hurt no more, but my jaw ached from biting the pillow.

That night at eleven o'clock, I met the surgeon, Dr. Hood. He was elected to biopsy a lymph node, and thus we would know my malady. I asked him to share with me the possible ramifications of the tumor. It was like he took a deck of cards called "Great Infirmities" out of his pocket and laid them before me:

INFIRMITY

Cancer of the lung	Hodgkin's disease	Cancer of lymphoid tissue	Leukemia	Tuberculosis

He left me with an assignment: to scrub the left side of my neck with betadine, an antiseptic solution.

I thought the right side might not look clean by contrast so I scrubbed my whole neck.

This was repeated in the morning, on the left side, by a nurse.

A stretcher came for me. Because of my pregnancy, I was allowed no narcotics to make it a twilight journey.

I was humming a little brave tune, but I was really overcome by the strangeness of the surgery corridor. The orderly seemed to step on a button, and *whoosh,* the doors opened into an odd country inhabited by people in green hats and baggy green shoes.

Before I could enter into my own surgery room, there seemed to be another admission form to fill out in addition to my signed consent slip. My identity was made verbally, then by hospital wristband, and operation schedule. I was asked a string of questions.

1. "Have your dentures been removed?"
   "I don't have any."
   We progressed to number ten. Allergies.
   "Do you really care if I'm allergic to dust and cat hair?"

But that was dutifully recorded.

After all the betadine preparations on the left side of my neck, Dr. Hood, without any obvious examination, had the nurse scrub the right side and cover me with sterile cloths. They covered my head and I could not see. As they began their incision, they laid their tools on my face. I didn't think I was going to be able to handle it, until words came to me like a standard in my mind:

> *That which is seen will pass away,*
> *that which is not seen is eternal.*

The conversation in the surgery room seemed so ludicrous; the nurses were talking about the cost of their new shoes. I was returned to my room feeling as if they had left a small tool inside my neck.

My next hurdle was waiting the days until the pathology report was complete. I found that the day shift lived by "proper procedure," and there were established guardians of rules and regulations. But the night shift was free, indeed. To some degree, I inverted my schedule: sleeping, as permitted, by day, and up at night.

The head night nurse gave me my chart to study, and I pored over all the comments and suggestions of what my illness might be. "Hodgkin's disease" was the most frequent notation, so I began to gather and learn all that I could, although my resources were limited to the floor library. I found a medical journal that outlined the indications of the disease's spread: the stages, the cell-type categories, and an outline of treatment. The article had two quotations which I memorized:

1. Pregnancy does not seem to affect the course of the disease.
2. The disease doesn't have any known effect on fertility, pregnancy, or on the children conceived by a parent with Hodgkin's disease.

I frequently did my reading in a doctor's anteroom, and there I had a confrontation with a young resident. He rebuked me for my study. He told me to stick to articles I could understand, like those in *Reader's Digest*. I wasn't even tolerant; I voted him Creep of the Week.

One morning during the family practice rounds, I told the doctors all I had learned about Hodgkin's, feeling like I was giving a talk to a college science class.

That afternoon, Dr. Hood came to see me. He had just received the laboratory report. He held my hand while telling me I had nodular-sclerosing Hodgkin's disease. He suggested I begin aggressive radiation therapy as soon as possible. But before the therapy began, it would be best, he stated, to have an abortion. I couldn't even consider an abortion, even with all his persuasive logic.

Later, Dr. Mainer came in with the same news. I told him that really I had been the very first to know.

The stitches were removed from my neck, and I was issued some medication because of a hazy urine culture. A nurse explained how this medication could cross the placental barrier. So I buried the pills in my hospital plants, and after I was discharged I let them rest unused in my home medicine chest.

HOSPITAL
OCT. 12

We learn obedience by the things that we suffer. On October 12, Sunday afternoon, I was readmitted through emergency with severe abdominal pain.

Sunday is not a day for doctors; Dr. Mainer had to come, just because of my call. Upon examination he said, "You have a rip-roaring urinary-tract infection." He asked if I had taken my prescription.

Oh, humble moment.

He could have yelled, pushed me off the table, and

told me what he had once planned for Sunday. But he exhibited true mercy. From that time, I always took my medication.

My outline for Monday was to go to ultrasound, a department where the gestational age of the baby could be indicated. But their equipment was temporarily out of order, so I was taken first to the radiation department. I was terrified. I felt I was being pushed in a little cattle car to Auschwitz, or some other extermination camp.

My fears all came upon me when I saw the corridor. I have never had an understanding of machines, small or great. Patients were treated behind lead-lined doors that read:

Red lights were turned on while technicians turned knobs, watching the cancer victims on TV screens.

I was taken into an examination room. I prayed

with utter fervor. There I had a vision in which my mind could see a story:

Naman was a Syrian who had leprosy. He sought a prophet of God who told him to dip seven times in the Jordan river, and he would be whole. Naman balked at the word; but he obeyed and was well.

There was much more than this, but it was clear to me that I had a course to follow, and in my submission to radiation, I would be restored.

I could face the staff with calmness. The plan was to start radiation treatments in what they called the high mediastinal field, delivering two thousand rads over a period of two and a half weeks.

It was still not an easy assignment. I was placed under an enormous cobalt machine. My imagination turned loose to a modern episode in *The Perils of Pauline,* an approaching science-fiction torment. I was alone and at war with my meditation.

Can one know my joy when the technicians returned with Dr. Mainer, halting the procedure until the ultrasound diagnosis was complete?

I jumped off the table, hopped on one foot, clapped my hands, refused the wheelchair transportation service, and went my way rejoicing.

I was interrupted at dinner, when a transportation-service orderly came to take me to ultrasound. There I lay on a cot as they covered my abdomen with oil, and with a gliding tool etched the infant within me on a screen. Their measurement estimated the gestational age at thirty-two weeks, in contrast to my own twenty-seven week calculation.

Because of the acceleration of the due-date, the therapeutic decision was now to postpone radiation until the baby was born. I was discharged with a pending follow-up appointment in the high-risk pregnancy clinic.

I was sick at home, but my family surrounded me. Our house is so small, I can be in bed and look into every room but one. So even in bed, I was in the bosom of my family.

Our agreement in marriage had always held to a strict division of labor. Richard did the man things, and I did the woman things, without crossing our streams. By necessity, Richard had begun to clean our house and cook our food. With great amazement, I rested on the couch and watched him cook dinner. Anything in life seemed possible. That was like turning the course of mighty rivers with a bare hand.

He had always been good with the children, but he increased in that capacity too. I would strain my ears to hear his bedtime serial stories of sailing ships, walking sticks, and trains. Bedtime was more than what had been my hasty guidance through toothbrush hygiene, so we were all enriched.

My symptoms got progressively worse. Night sweats drenched me. I was so short of breath that I could not read aloud, and I could hardly sing. Still, I coughed, although "Red Bomb," my cough syrup, reduced the rack of it to lower-case letters. Going to the doctor was my chorus; it repeated itself after every verse in my life.

During one visit to the clinic I was asked if I would make a videotape in the basement of Emma Jones Hall.

I had been feeling like a soap-opera star through all the suspended decisions. I could hum violin music, look at the wall, and invite everyone to tune in again tomorrow.

I asked the nurse about the tape. She replied, "It will probably be used in the death-and-dying series in the nursing and medical school studies."

"Oh," I answered, sobered.

The day of the taping Dr. Mainer took me down the stairs into an illuminated room.

I sat in a news-room chair across from a pleasant-seeming man whose gray hair was crew-cut. When the interview started he changed before me into a machine that ejected hard balls for me to bat answers back to. It was alive with high fastballs and curves. My inquirer was without mercy. He kept my mind swinging.

Finally he said, "Is there anything you would like to know?"

"Yes. Who are you?" I asked.

He was the kind who answers questions with questions. "Who have you heard that I am?"

"Dr. Tollhouse," I said.

"That is close," said Dr. Taubman.

Later Dr. Mainer explained that he was the staff psychiatrist.

Then I had perfect understanding of why the world calls them "shrinks." My brain collapsed the rest of the day from his probing.

He seemed ever-learning and never-understanding.

I followed my appointment in the OB clinic with Dr. Montoya, the chief resident. He looked like a pizza baron. He wore a tomato-sauce tie. He threw his words up and out, baking everything with the intensity of his expression. He went through every progressing abdominal measurement and date and concluded ultrasound was right. I had a little calendar that marked my last period, which would still put me in the six-month chute. I spoke what I felt was true, but I felt more concerned for the baby than myself. Thus, I was relieved when Dr. Montoya confirmed that they would use a drug to induce labor as soon as the infant had sufficiently matured. This induction would supersede radiation therapy.

I was also seeing Dr. Mainer, who agreed with my calculations, but we flowed with the more expert opinion. I had weekly chest X rays which showed that the tumor was enlarging, and the lymph nodes were increasing in size.

As much as I thrilled to Richard's help, there was one drawback. He didn't cook with a great repertoire. For breakfast we always had very hard eggs; the yolk could support a fork in a vertical position. This was accompanied by a helping of pork and beans. Dinner was mostly hamburgers with very boiled vegetables and a lettuce wedge.

I began to lose my appetite and thought it was a

symptom of progressive disease. Then one day I just didn't feel like swallowing any more.

I shared this with Dr. Mainer by telephone. He said, "This is worrisome."

LAUREL'S
$20.00 STOVE

HOSPITAL
OCT. 31

Following Dr. Mainer's orders, I was admitted into the hospital that same Friday night. Dr. Steve Fredrickson was on call. I had never met him, but was advised he would be my weekend attending physician.

He came into the room, and I said, "You must be Dr. Fredrickson."

He said, "Just call me Steve."

It usually takes so long for a doctor to drop his occupational manner with a patient, and share anything personal. But Steve was first a person, and used the doctors' vocabulary only when relevant. I noticed another thing too: He was the first doctor whose classic black bag was not embossed with his title in gold letters. Personalness removes strangeness, and is a comfort.

A patient is continually exposed to groups of medical students and department specialists. I found I could classify doctors into three styles of patient management:

1. The doctor who shares only the very immediate: that present moment.
2. The doctor who shares the next step, and explains in some detail its construction.
3. The doctor who points to the vast landscape ahead, showing not only bridges and cities but every possible avenue.

There are always exceptions. I had one fourth-year student from hematology who told me glibly I had five years to live. I could laugh at him because I knew my disease and knew I knew more about it than he did. I had continued to study Hodgkin's disease, reading from books and current journals to protect myself from every wind and doctrine of doctors. I also wanted more understanding to refute my imaginings when I felt so sick and fading.

This was my third time in the hospital. In addition to the other symptoms, my admittance sheet stated: "Onset of dysphagia." The progress report was more graphic: "Today intake has been minimal, but patient noticed difficulty in swallowing, with sensation of food becoming 'hung-up' in throat."

I was scheduled for a barium swallow to see if the tumor was affecting my esophagus. Simultaneously, the nurses made summaries on their page: ". . . complained of being hungry. . . ." Another noted ". . . ate well at breakfast and lunch, requested double orders."

I realized it was Richard's cooking that had precipitated my hospitalization. I felt trapped, forced to walk through yet another bull ring. The humor of the circumstance was apparent to me too. I wadded the ludicrousness of it up and stuffed it in my hospital-gown pocket.

I continued to make primitive observations. The surgeon wanted to abort, the radiologist wanted radiation, and the OB specialist was concerned for the infant. Can this be the essence of the multidisciplinarian approach? It must be too simple a generalization.

November 1, Saturday

I was taken to the site where barium swallows are administered. I had to stand between machines, and was given a cup of thick, white fluid. Nothing could have prepared me for such a horrible taste, and I gagged and spewed it from my mouth. The technician was very serious when he asked if this was how I swallowed. I braced myself for the cup, and managed to get the barium down. There was little evidence of obstruction.

I was transferred to the OB floor, where there were a number of women with high-risk pregnancies. But the majority were young mothers who would come and go. There was such evidence of joy among the delivered citizens. I was always sighing within myself that everything would go well for me.

It was a terrible way to spend a Sunday morning. I was transported to diagnostic ultrasound, where their etching device located a pocket of amniotic fluid. By extracting a sample of this water, the lab could determine the maturity of the fetal lungs.

The package of tools for the tap looked medieval. I felt like a picture in a sequence of the history of medicine. But wherever you are, there you are, and it was done.

The lab report was returned, marked "immature." Examination determined the fetal size to be a mere four pounds.

Somehow Dr. Mainer had begun to concur with Dr. Montoya that the gestational age was now thirty-five weeks. I knew it was thirty weeks and even argued with Dr. Montoya in a dream.

Ambassadors from all the specialized countries of medicine came to see me and to examine my culture with their varied proposals of aid. They had a United

Nations meeting to decide my governing treatment policies. Delegates came from hematology, neonatal pediatrics, family practice, and the OB service. They were moving to the conference room. I felt it was my right to go.

From an access closet by the delivery corridor I removed a full doctor's outfit and dressed myself, disguising the bulk of Laurel into what I hoped looked like another doctor who could deliver a baby. Only my eyes showed through the headgear. I planned to grab a metal chart board and hang around the door.

Alas, Dr. Montoya found me touching up the last of my costume. He sent me soundly to bed. He said, "You can't go because we yell at these meetings." And I bet they take off their shoes and pound them too.

The hematology staff chief had given me a bedside discourse. At the conclusion of his talk he asked his colleague, Dr. Bagby, to share his perceptions with the group: "Immediate radiation therapy is required as further encroachment on the superior vena cava will endanger the life of the mother and the fetus . . ."

When we were little children, we played a little game called "telephone." We would sit in a circle. One would whisper some news to the one next to him. And around and around would this little word be passed until the last to receive it would speak what he heard. We would laugh at how it had been jumbled.

The progression of the hematologist's words from my bedside to the group, through Dr. Montoya, and back to me varied not in one jot or phrase. I was not ignorant of the danger of radiation to the fetus. Dr. Montoya had been emphatic about the chance of retardation.

Tears just welled in my eyes, and that was another heavy little corner in the afternoon at the medical school.

November 4

I girded my mind and went to radiation therapy. They were unable to obtain my progressive X rays, and no one from radiation therapy had been able to attend the conference. A staff member examined me and stated he was not convinced I was really in need of radiation. In consideration of the pending due-date, he felt that the decision to initiate therapy was completely mine, and I should consider it well.

Transportation was called and I was returned to my room.

I was in real stress. All men were liars. If I had had any strength, I would have run away for the afternoon just to look at one solid thing, like a tree.

They called for me again. They had located my X rays. Those pictures had crossed out all the radiologist's morning words. The radiation began at once. The betatron machine was chosen, because it emitted the least scatter.

I was rolled under its girth. Earphones were applied because the machine roared as it worked. They put

small rice bags on my neck, and a lead apron over my
abdomen. I could feel the baby moving within me and
my mind was held constant to God.

The day of the second treatment, peace of mind
rolled slowly back up and filled me. I spent the hours
of that returning tide with my water colors, painting
a little picture. I recalled the lines from Isaiah:

> When thou walkest through the fire,
> thou shall not be burned,
> neither shall the flame be kindled upon thee.

My days lay in bed, except for the radiation call.
I cranked the hospital cot up as high as it would go,
to give my eye the best of the panorama from my window. I watched the movement of the city and the progression of the sky. Sometimes boats pulled logs, bound
in chains, up the Willamette River. It was a provision
for my spirit.

"WHEN THOU WALKEST THROUGH THE FIRE, THOU SHALT NOT BE BURNED NEITHER SHALL THE FLAME BE KINDLED UPON THEE." ISAIAH 43:2

The nurse's note read: "Patient prefers to have bed all the way up. Refuses to let me roll it down. Climbs in and out of bed with help of chair. Was told how dangerous this was. R.N. Notified."

On the second floor the nurses' notes hung at the end of the bed. But the OB floor policy was to enclose them in an inaccessible chart. I found if a nurse was conscious that the notes were available to the patient, it produced one kind of recording of physical movements. The notations tucked within a chart held at the desk were another style, often dealing with their perception of the patient's emotional realm.

I found what seemed like tender concern from a nurse would elicit my tender confidence, only to find it distorted and recorded for the hospital world. I felt betrayed and limited their probes to the external.

Some notes made me sound a little insane: "At 0500 still awake and ravenously eating an orange—short of breath . . . no complaints." Another: "Poor breakfast. States, 'Not hungry,' had milk and juice. Saves food from the trays and places on window ledge and in drawer. States, 'Hate to waste food.' "

The OB floor could swarm with a great influx, until they would even put patients in the supply room. One Friday the rooms were crowded with extra beds.

I prevailed upon Dr. Mainer for a weekend pass. I had missed my little children so greatly. In my transportation to radiation, I would ride through the out-patient pediatric clinic and ache through that track, seeing the small faces.

I went home and we were all precious together. Everything had so much color. Richard kept our old wood stove so stocked with lumber that the corner of the house was of a tropical warmth.

Matthew found in a plastic bag of fruit one more mottled than the rest. "Look Mom, it's got Hodgkin's disease."

Anna is only three. She would climb on my lap, dragging my old yellow bathrobe, rubbing its nylon lining and sucking her fingers.

In its sweetness was a sadness too. I felt I was carrying an hourglass of our fleeting time together. I dragged my feet all the way back to the hospital.

My roommate of the previous week had had a cold, and I had breathed in her sneezes. At home what was tropical by night was arctic by morning. By Tuesday, November 11, I had bronchitis. I had severe chest pain which warred against my cough center:

> "I must cough" versus "No, that's real pain."
> As they locked in combat;
> I couldn't even breathe . . .

The tumor was swelling from radiation in its own death process, and I had great shortness of breath. They hung an oxygen water-fountain box above my bed. They fastened this pure air into me with nose prongs.

I kept thinking, if the urban air pollution continues, we'll all be wearing some kind of portable unit in a few years.

A university hospital is a learning institution, where the young students are reared to become old and wise doctors. Dr. Bagby brought a class of students into my room. He had me sit in a chair. He moved a stethoscope across my back and had me continually pronounce the letter *E*. As I understood him, he was explaining how this letter *E* would sound like the letter *A* as it crossed the chest mass.

Then it was the students' turn. One by one, I continually made the letter *E* for them. I blew *E*s out in the air. I became hysterical in my imagination. I felt we were making a tape for a preschool show on the alphabet. I thought I turned into a Cheshire cat, and that was all I could say. I couldn't bear the absurdity and began to say, in the same tone of voice, the letter *A*. No one even noticed. We had all gone insane.

Doctors and patients are at two elevations. I knew everyone by their belt buckles. They were subtle, mid-line bumper stickers. I read them in profusion.

There was the grass roots category with metal marijuana leaves. Mike Mainer wore a stylized eagle. One doctor friend had a Mickey Mouse head. It seemed that the minority had simple squares, just functional, without a style.

I was always meeting new doctors. Dr. Leslie Dillow came into my room reading my chart. After some study she asked, "Didn't it hurt to turn thirty?" I was so used to objective questions that I had to really think if I had had any special symptomatic problems on my birthday.

Directly after radiation on November 13, I was taken to ultrasound, where Dr. Dillow performed another amniocentesis. I was disturbed because the baby was moving within me. A good-sized needle was inserted in the amniotic sac, and the fluid was extracted. Dr. Dillow exclaimed that she could feel the baby kicking the needle, and I was very upset when I saw that the sample was not clear, but bloody. I thought the baby had been pierced by the needle.

Within myself, I was incensed. I refused to wait for the wheelchair service and walked back to my room. I knew the evidence obtained was important, but the means seemed as primitive as when they used leeches in medicine shows. Then my ward nurse told me how last year a fetus went into intrauterine shock when the cord was inadvertently pierced. I raged.

An order came forth for me to come into the labor room and be fastened into an abdominal belt to measure fetal heart tones. As the ticker paper rolled out onto the floor, it was within normal limits, except at random there were utterly irregular, abnormal-looking scratches. It seemed like the baby was having cardiac arrests. I took the strip back to my room. The floor doctor rested me with his words. The bloody tap was the result merely of nicking a blood vessel in the placenta. The scratchings that seemed like heart failures were ordinary fetal movement.

Machines give me screams when I don't understand.
Give me the answers in this doctors'-man land.

The view from my window, which had been my sustaining friend, turned into a great enemy. Its message was my separation from my family. It spoke louder to me each day. I would yell at the window and out of the window: "Willamette River, you may as well be the Mississippi for as near as I am to home."

The chart didn't record homesickness, but I began to suffer this malady of separation. I had never had this disorder before. I would find myself thinking of our little house with the vines growing over the front porch. There is a stained-glass window hanging over an antique couch, given to me once while I was walking to the grocery store. I spent my mind on such details.

When Dr. Mainer made his rounds in the morning, I told him in solemn tones, "I've lost my will to live," pause, "in the hospital."

On November 14, I completed 1700 rads of radiation. On November 17, the X ray showed that the tumor was shrinking. That afternoon a man whom I had never seen before came into my room to state that I could be discharged that day.

Good-bye for now, and another plastic identification wristband was cut away and disposed of.

I was put on a schedule of once-a-week visits to Dr. Mainer, who now concurred with my original due-date for the baby. It was decided to let me go full term as a result of a hematology and radiation consultation.

I had a fur coat that was once my mother's; it became my winter pleasure. One December doctor's visit Matthew hatched a plot as we waited in the examination room. He turned off the light and it was very black.

He waited on his hands and knees behind the examination table. He wrapped his animal stature in my fur.

"Well," said Dr. Mainer. "What's this?" upon finding such a dark room. With a ferocious growl Matthew crawled out to attack the physician.

Dr. Mainer reached the light switch and the rest of our time was routine.

I respected Mike Mainer immensely. I was always a person-patient with him first, not just another case. This was based on a feeling, not words.

It was rare for our conversation to go beyond what was medically relevant. He kept disclosures of his inner self on a strict budget.

I was told once that the residents make twelve thousand dollars a year. That sounded like Tarzan's ivory horde to me.

When Mike Mainer told me he frequently moonlights in the emergency room, I was surprised. I knew he worked an abundance of hours as a third-year resident. I apologized for being bold and rude but suggested that free time for walking in mountains was sweeter than gold.

"Buy clothes in a thrift store for a change," I said.

He laughed but replied that school loans were due.

We left his office and went to the cafeteria. He asked me to sit with him. He was wearing a genuine World War II leather flight jacket and a "thank you for not smoking" pin. He asked me about how I had become a Christian.

"I was in a wooden cabin built on the back of a pick-up truck en route to Alaska to homestead. It was nine years ago. I had been at Berkeley. Timothy Leary was at Harvard. I was a psychedelic inner-space pioneer on one of the first flights to the moon of enlightenment. It was made of cheese.

"I deduced that illumination was gradual, a kind of growth into the light, like all the vegetables I was going to plant in my garden.

"Instead, I was born again."

Mike looked at me and said, "I once was a lot happier. I want to get back there again."

I increased in bulk in December. I was so pregnant that even when empty seats were available on the bus, people would spring up and offer me theirs too. I knew

January 22, 1967

45

I would probably never have another child, and even those enlarged, uncomfortable days were put on special tapes in my mind. I only heard one line for the "Christmas Story": "And she was great with child . . ." (Luke).

My official due-date was New Year's Eve, December 31, and it was arranged for me to be induced at this time. As I left for the hospital, I gave the baby basket a last look. It had been a strange forest I had carried the child through.

Richard and the children drove me to the hospital, with the children singing all the way, "This is the day, this is the day." They dropped me off at the hospital's north door with final instructions: Matthew wanted a boy, and Anna wanted a girl. Neither cared what color the baby was.

It was standing room only in the labor room. Others must have had tax exemptions to worry about. I had to be rescheduled. I rode the bus home, glad for two more days.

Richard said, "What are you doing here?"

I said, "It wasn't the day after all."

On New Year's Day, I took the children roller skating on the sidewalk. I pulled them along and held them up at the same time. How we feel can be just like a wind of weather; I was happy. I was full of life, in me, around me, on each arm.

HOSPITAL
JANUARY 2

I went to the hospital admissions department; I called it the "booking room" under my breath. Everything in hospitals always begins with questions. By now everyone in the office seemed to know me. A nurse took me to the OB delivery and labor suite. Mike Mainer and I met at 8:00 A.M. "Good," he said, because he is a man of schedule.

My assigned labor bed was under a window, and Mount Hood was visible that day. An amniotic hook

48

was used to break the membranes and because this might also stimulate natural labor.

Then I was surrounded and attached, plugged into and connected to machines.

The first baby born in outer space.

A fetal heart-monitor belt was buckled. An abdominal contraction belt was buckled. I had an IV, and a special box that seemed to have a green flashing light. At 10:45 they began the drip of pitocin, or "induce-juice." My body believed it and began to make contractions.

The abdominal contraction belt transmitted the tremors to a graph I could watch. It was like a child's drawing of hills on a strip that would roll out and pile up on the floor. The baby had its own paper recording its own heart.

Having once lived on the OB floor for two weeks, I had friends among the staff. They came and sat with me through labor. The machines were at my front, and my sisters gathered around my back. The floor doctor asked if I had ever been induced before. For some reason I thought he asked if I had ever been *seduced* before. We all laughed, and the humanness overcame the machines. It felt like a home delivery.

At 1 o'clock, I had dilated 6 centimeters. A scalp electrode was applied to the baby's head, and there were more wires. At 1:20, I was given oxygen through nasal prongs.

When the contractions reflected on the graph looked

the same as Mount Hood, I closed my eyes. Richard came and held my hand. The contractions intensified. My sisters applied pressure to my lower back.

At 2:15, I was rolled into the delivery room and everyone came with me. Mike Mainer dashed in, just in time.

I was permeated with a sense that all was in order, and my mind seemed to expand to the universal of women having children, not in any time-space sequence, but from the beginning to the end. The baby crowned; I kept forgetting to watch the mirror.

At 2:35, Mary Elisabeth was born, instantly cried, and the roomful of adults seemed to move back a generation.

My sisters moved with me down the hall. They knocked at the nursery door, and the baby was held up. She weighed almost nine pounds. They all exclaimed in the talk of women. I felt I could run the length and breadth of the world.

I was moved into a postpartum room where one nurse delighted in pushing my abdomen. I understood the "uterus-shrink" principle, but she maneuvered as if she were in a great contest to press all the air out of an air mattress.

It was the original birthday party, and my eyes could see balloons pinned to the ceiling, and it seemed there should be cake on the dinner tray. I was given the same window berth in Hospitalization No. 4 as in my previous captivity.

Some infant formula company had given the hospital a sign which was put in the hallway, prohibiting visitors. They would wheel down the babies in long trains of portable beds.

They brought my baby for the first time with instructions not to nurse her until she had been given sterile water. Newborns are like birds puckering their faces; something's about to come. I nursed her. A mother with her infant has had to be painted by every generation.

Saturday and Sunday Mary Elisabeth was mine for a brief season, with a circle just around us, and all the cares to come had to recede.

Mike Mainer had gone on a vacation, and Steve Fredrickson was my overseeing physician. I had more than a new mother's schedule.

I thought: so short the rest, so often the test.

Monday, January 5, 1976

En route to nuclear medicine, the wheelchair driver snatched my chart away and carried it himself, not to lead me into temptation. I only wanted to distract my journey with nurses' notes, which can sometimes provide four-line comedy relief.

The nuclear medicine department has its permission forms to sign too, with their twentieth-century seal.

I was injected with radioactive isotopes so that a liver-spleen scan could be performed. One of the doctors stretched me out on a table. I could watch my liver and spleen glisten on a wall screen as if they were loaded with Mexican jumping bean gold-dust.

On the other side of the room, another patient was placed on a table and the technician took a shuttle and passed it back and forth over her body. She kept pleading for water, in a way that made the word sound like six syllables. I thought, "So this is what it's like to make a James Bond movie."

They would give me no sign of what the test revealed.

I was instructed to wear a lead apron when I held my baby. I had to use a formula for a given period of time and discard my breast milk.

1. The baby is wheeled in.
2. I have to wash with an antiseptic cloth, turning the first smell of mother into a deodorizer.
3. I'm girded with a lead apron, adding forty pounds to my postpartum weight.
4. I'm given a bottle with a whole list of ingredients . . .
5. My breasts say, "Now what's the matter?"
   I use a breast pump that looks like a bicycle horn.

Who cares? She is a healthy baby. But I want the doctors to confirm that with me.

Upper-mantle radiation treatments were scheduled to be resumed, and I want to know if I can be simmered by rads and still nurse Mary Elisabeth. A note was written requesting a conference with a neonatal pediatrician and Mary Elisabeth's mother.

In the meantime, in between time, I was wheeled early in the morning to diagnostic X ray for a lymphangiogram. Machines hung from the ceiling on tracks, and I sat on a table beneath these mechanical webs.

I manually expressed the baby's feeding, which seemed quite disconcerting to the technician. But she overcame her discomfiture, and explained the lymphangiogram procedure. Dye would be inserted through a small incision in between my toes and channeled into my lymphatic system; when absorbed, the X-ray series would show any abnormality.

The staff physician of the department came in to view the opening procedure. I mentioned that I had just had a baby four days ago. She asked me about the delivery, but the words she wanted to use escaped her. Instead, she made a cutting movement with her finger, and an appropriate cutting noise as a way of inquiring. I replied that I had had an episiotomy in the delivery. She rescheduled the lymphangiogram for January 13.

The neonatal pediatrician came to see me. He was the original Dr. Elevator-Driver, who pushed the button for the "photography" floor on that first real day. Stu Levy has a face one cannot fully forget and one cannot fully know because it is full of hair like the burning bush, but the flame is in the eyes.

Our second encounter is framed and hung on a wall back in my mind. In speaking of Mary Elisabeth, he said the words from the book of Daniel, without knowing it: "After examining her . . . she appears more vigorous than the rest . . ."

I felt I could levitate on the bed, and Stu asked,

"Just what are you into, anyway?"

One can choke with the joy of a joke that is never said. I wanted to reply, "The American Girl Scouting Movement," but I swallowed the line.

"Jesus," I said.

He asked me if I had ever heard of Richard Alpert.

"Yes," I said, "I heard him lecture in Haight-Ashbury ten years ago. All I remember is that he admonished us to get some psilocybin, because of the realms of love to which it elevated the inner man."

Stu went on to say that Alpert had gone to India and found a ragged "holy man" who was being worshiped. Alpert wondered at this until the man revealed the secrets of Alpert's heart, and Alpert embraced him too.

Oh beggarly elements. Alpert took the wrong trail. There is one way. I am adamant. I had to hush myself, for in saying too much, nothing is heard.

I had some of the usual postpartum problems. I was constipated. In Steve Fredrickson's rounds, I shared my complaint. It took courage for me to broach such private business with Steve. Sometimes invoking the word *doctor* can pull a mask over the clinician's face; like when the imitation glasses are attached to the plastic nose with a moustache ruffle. I didn't have that prop with Steve.

He prescribed a common, bad-tasting remedy and roused me from sleep the next morning with jokes about the medicine's effect. Often the way up is down, but I had no mental set for what I considered a delicate topic. Let self-reproach and remorse come later; I kicked his leg twice. But friends can take such abuse, where a doctor and a patient can't.

I went home that day, and he put a whole pint bottle in my medicine discharge sack.

I dressed the baby, myself, for the first time. The nurse carried her to the car. It's a state law. We carried the load of samples that all the infant-supplies manufacturers want associated with the newborn's nurture.

A song of the family is sharing the new one with the brother and the sister. Anna had triumphed in the fact that we had had a daughter. Richard told me that she stuffed dolls up her shirt during my five-day stay. Then she would whip them out, exclaiming, "It's a girl!" to Matthew's continual chagrin. My son came and peered through all the January blankets. "Well, she looks just like a boy." So the unity of the spirit was now maintained in the bond of peace.

As for me, as we rode home from the hospital, I was dancing on the roof of the car, figuratively speaking.

I was not an untried mother. I fully knew that an infant takes more maintaining than just being arranged in Carter's new layette. The baby's up at night, the little children are up by day.

Sleep is an illusion, a mirage. As one attempts to act upon it, as if it were a reality, it only vanishes in trying to seize it.

I was like a robot performing every function from rote memory. It's a perfect self-denial, a baptism that can change girls to women in that exhausting underwater swim.

There were night watches when the baby would not stop crying. I often thought: The world needs a gifted chemist to put another concoction in an aerosol can. "Baby Hush" could be sprayed at bedside to produce instant sleep.

There were nights I imagined deep in my pillow I was nailing boards between myself and the sound. I would hammer planks over the wail, trying to build a quiet box to sleep in.

I wonder if a lone Chinese mother ever thought of acupuncture.

On January 13, I returned for the lymphangiogram. It's strange to watch dye and oil going through your toes being absorbed into your system. I asked how long these chemicals would be in my body. "Oh, for years," said the technician.

There was a screen that separated me from a man undergoing the same procedure. Our names were on a blackboard where the times and amounts of fluid were recorded. At random, X rays were taken to check the absorption rate. It was like we were in a contest to see who could be set free first. My feet and body ached to move, but under great penalty of loosening their devices and thus repeating the ordeal. I fell in and out of low blankets of sleep, rigid.

I won over the other contestant, and he groaned. Then I stood, and bent, and rolled, and inhaled and exhaled for the first series of X rays. It was a very strange way to spend the day; even my urine was blue.

Early the next morning the telephone rang, and I ran to the ring to keep it from sounding. I wanted to keep the children asleep, and I juggled noises with schedules to keep it all moving. But I started to bleed—filling the floor, a mess by the door.

I sat down. Matthew got up, and took in the scene. "Well, thank God you didn't do that on the Oriental rug." That five-year-old perception started me laughing.

HOSPITAL
JANUARY
14

Later that morning I had to take the children and divide them all into different houses. It's sad that the Lee family pie was again cut into pieces and distributed. There is a whole language in sighs. I felt locked into hospitals.

A medical chart is just data plus data plus data. The information from the previous tests was available. The liver-spleen report stated, "Spleen appears mildly enlarged, with a mottled liver." I didn't bend and fold on hearing this, as most medical authorities don't consider the liver-spleen scan significant in regard to Hodgkin's disease. And the lymphangiogram, which *is* regarded as relevant, was normal.

It was my night to sleep, sweet and deep. "It's my only chance," I told the nurse.

She was zealous for blood. She kept coming with a flashlight to look for stains. She was trained to read red spots like tea leaves.

It was determined that a placenta fragmentation had been retained and was discharged in the initial bleeding.

I was discharged too. I felt like a bird that had escaped from the snare of the fowler.

Hospital, hospital, number five,
one day later, I'm out alive.

I had to have the stitches from the lymphangiogram taken out of my feet. I went to the family practice clinic.

When Life Gives You Lemons, Make Lemonade

Steve Fredrickson took off my shoes and socks. As he kneeled and bent over my foot he pretended he was a shoe salesman.

"What size shoe do you wear? What kind are you interested in today?" He waved to indicate a stockroom that before our imagination began was just a row of hospital gowns.

"Oh, I want the kind with tiny heels and pointed toes."

He acted dismayed. "Those are really out of style now."

"I know," I replied, "but they are the best for kicking doctors."

After that sentence he became a regular physician; a visiting medical student just stared at us.

I resumed the wife-and-mother hike, but I was wearing a backpack that had cast-iron pans in its sack. As an outpatient I went for treatment every day. Radiation was initiated on the upper mantle with the intent of delivering 4,000 rads in eight weeks. It was an uphill climb.

At 1 P.M., the infant, the children, and I would enter the radiation hall. The department head, Dr. Moss, once remarked, "We only see a nursing mother once every five years." Sometimes I would emerge from the treatment room to find my children darting on stools with wheel bases in between the stretchers and wheelchairs.

The path had such steep rocks. Within myself I was so exhausted that life lost all its colors, its past, and its future. I was pressed down by each day.

The radiation field was etched on my chest with red ink. Within the target area were outlines of my lungs. Lead blocks were built to protect those organs.

At home Anna took a red flow pen to make lines on her own chest to be like her mother. The children were exposed to more than I could bear myself. They played doctor an inordinate amount, making a doctor's office behind the couch. There they would take their stuffed animals to an invisible Dr. Mainer, who seemed to live back there for a while. The diagnosis was simple; everything either had Hodgkin's disease or a cold. Matthew sometimes was the physician himself. He used a chain and a lot of wet Kleenex in his treatments.

They helped my perception: *Bum thoughts could*

come looking for a handout.

On the top of the hill was a veterans' hospital. It had American flags at the front entrance, unlike hospital North and hospital South.

Every afternoon a van brought the veterans over to the radiation department for treatment. They came the same time in the afternoon that I did and I knew their faces.

Greyhound bus drivers honk at each other while passing on the highway. Women with tiny children the same age smile at each other in supermarkets. The veterans and I had cancer; it put us in one fraternity.

Once I followed them through the lobby of the hospital; old men in brown-and-white striped bathrobes.

There was a murmuring behind them after they passed.

"Did you see those red marks on them? It's for the radiation machines."

It's like they were passing lepers and everyone whispered, "Unclean, unclean."

I hurried and got in the elevator with them and we all rode up to the fourth floor together.

Among the younger patients I had one blood brother named Carl, and one blood sister named Darlene. We all had Hodgkin's disease.

They were treated in the morning and if I ever chanced upon them, we would hug on sight.

I grew accustomed to the look of the radiation department. The fact that there were snowballs in stretchers who had almost finished their roll down their hill didn't make me wince. I could finally look into a melting face. It was just real.

The mothers with the sick little children were the hardest for me. They were always perfectly tender with their injured ones, who needed no tether; they didn't move.

I kept feeling a cosmic apology that mine had to emphasize the contrast of health. Anna loved to climb the coat rack to the top. The other mothers were at the other end of my tunnel. Their child was leaving them; I was leaving my children.

> Where are words
> That say good-bye
> I'm just going
> I will not die
> I think it best
> To shout it out:
> *See you later*
> *alligator*
> *After a while,*
> *crocodile.*

Sometimes due to an influx of patients or a mechanical failure we had hours to wait on the turquoise blue plastic couches. Matthew and Anna would always dare a standing broad jump and measure their flight by squares of linoleum. The office personnel would stiffen their faces into they-could-get-hurt looks.

Magazines became more than a turning page. They had found all the trains and animals the first time. They could line them up on the floor, etching in glossy color a boat. The rest of us in the waiting room had wet feet. Purses were fish.

The employees of the radiation therapy department were in three categories: the doctors, the technicians who operated the machines, and the office workers. With such a grim casualty rate, they took release in celebrations. They marked staff birthdays with wild tribute to the sugar industry. They would transform their employee table into a grandiose pot-luck confectionary. I had been there so long I was ushered into their inner sweet circle. Under the influence of so many diet admonitions, it seemed to me a shocking display of sugar castles. Anna called them "yummie crummies." One doctor confided they gave him two birthdays in one year. There was never one raw cauliflower on a toothpick. *Let every man be fully persuaded in his own mind.*

My strength was breaking down into half-lives. My body was in rebellion. My lot became the baby and the couch, while Richard had to resume care for the rest of the ranch. When he had to work late, I was helpless as the effect of the treatments accumulated. With my authority weak, it was like the sheriff had left town, and it was wild West days for the children.

One evening I told Matthew to get some granola cereal. As I moved in and out of consciousness, they decided to play cows and poured the cereal all over the table. Cows don't use spoons or bowls. Then, it occurred to Matthew that cows don't eat off tables. So they poured their nutritious flakes all over the floor and ate them, mooing on their hands and knees.

What a sight to bless a mother's weary heart.

It was time to bring more authority into town. One call to my mother put her on the afternoon plane.

We were all in subjection now to the fastest gun, and order reigned. To further ease the exhaustion, my mother was going to take Mary Elisabeth home with her.

I was warned that the upper-field lung blocks were originally calculated on the simulator for my girth as a nursing mother. Thus, I could not wean the baby without threat to my lungs. I wanted my mother to stay as long as she could to keep from having to use manual expression to maintain a nursing mother's dimension. And more than that, it's very hard to see your little baby fly off to California for an unknown period of time.

But Mother had her airplane reservations and was eager to fly back to a comfortable twentieth-century house with her bundle. Besides, her girl friends were planning a shower.

We made an appointment for a complete pediatric check-out before the flight. The family practice clinic got three generations. Steve Fredrickson was temporarily replacing Mike Mainer in looking after us.

Before being ushered into the examination room, I found Steve peering through his glasses into a microscope and shared in brief my situation.

Dr. Fredrickson did such a thorough examination of the newborn. A rash and a stuffy nose elicited great concern. He asked if my mother could remain until this was stable, simultaneously giving my leg a tap.

A few days later I finished radiation on the upper mantle. I nursed the baby for the last time, then Richard drove Mother to the airport. Matthew and I sat and cried and hugged each other. He had decided that Mary Elisabeth was his very favorite.

The night Mary Elisabeth flew to California my friends had a baby shower for me. I opened a pile of miniature clothes which were passed around the circle of ladies.

oh, goodbye for now

We made limericks as a contest. The winner was
Kate Carson:

> There once was a baby named Mary
> Whose days in the womb were quite scary
> She had a rough time
> But she came out fine
> And now all the saints are so merry!

We ate cake, cutting a glazed, healthy stork into
squares.

My friends were well-lighted houses where I could
go and rest along my way.

Four inches of hair fell out as a result of the radiation treatments. It filled my brush; I piled it on the
floor. My neck looked like someone had put a bowl on
my head and shaved across. I had an inverted receding
hairline. When I tried to braid it my nakedness made
me look like I was wearing a cheap wig a size smaller
than my head.

There had been some question among the radiation therapy doctors in regard to removing my spleen. This is a routine procedure for determining the stage of Hodgkin's disease.

The fulcrum of the consideration was in the preservation of the ovarian function, as the ovaries could be moved to midline and shielded during the lower-mantle radiation. Thus, I would not be thrust into menopause. On the other hand, it could be an unnecessary major surgery and the doctors reported certain possible problems once a spleen was removed.

I tried to manage my own decision, wading through a series of medical school generalizations. Everyone I asked had a concise laparotomy lecture. I took my question off the bookshelf and asked the faculty what they themselves would do. Again, some said yes and some said no. I entered carrying a black-and-white question and left holding every possible shade of gray.

I called Mike Mainer and packed together this great gray ball of considerations and rolled it to him. He decided on the laparotomy, and I had peace. It was nice to just be able to think in four-line poems again.

There was a very short span between the completion of upper-mantle radiation and my scheduled surgery. I would say, "Stomach, you'll never look this good again. . . ."

HOSPITAL
FEBRUARY 29

I was admitted under surgery's banner. The greeting orderly put me in a ward with four beds in a tight row. As he wrote his "white female admitted, ambulatory" introduction, he asked me how to spell "disease." The lady in the next bed was testing the smoke sensitivity device in the ceiling by keeping her hot cigarettes rolling.

"Please move me," I said. I was taken across the hall and put in a two-bed room under the window.

One of the surgery team members came in, identified himself, and began an examination. He left the room, and another man came in and asked the same kind of questions, and gave me the same kind of examination. As he left the room I thought it was odd, but when a third came with the same procedure it seemed to be very funny—and it might be very disorganized. I did not want the surgery department disorganized. But they all came back together: it was the admission plan.

I had two days before my operation. I was offered every color of jello and every flavor of bouillon cube. I fasted, and embroidered a bird on an old coat.

A hospital patient can have a multitude of roommates. A certain quality of the hospital experience is in that particular interaction. There are a lot of different kinds of animals in the hospital ark.

I had roommates so young on the OB floor that they were back in the part of the world that sighs over rock-'n'-roll stars.

I had a roommate so old the nurses and I called her gramma, and she ached in every direction.

I once thought they brought a man in to share my room, complete with tattoos and after-shave lotion. He was a she, with cancer of the uterus; she was tough by day, but cried at night.

I had one roommate who would flip her front teeth out and then draw them back with her tongue. She talked all the time in streams without reason.

There were sweet little sisters, and ladies whose years had bent them into ways that were their own.

I now had a new roommate whose legs were healing from donating skin to a mastectomy wound. Her name was Clara; she was wise and kind and clear. She had spent her years as a pastor's wife in rural Wyoming towns.

She told me wonderful stories about western ranch life, but she was quiet in quiet times too.

There are groups within groups. No one knows from where the wind blows or where it goes.

Somehow I heard of a Bible study held every Tuesday morning at seven in the hospital South cafeteria. It was led by Dr. Ritzman, the chief of staff of the cardiac division, with his wife, a doctor also. They prayed for me; they knew of my pending operation the following morning.

The head of the radiation department, Dr. William T. Moss, is a most eminent man. Not only is he a frequent speaker at medical conventions, but he has written three textbooks which have been widely distributed in schools for the study of radiation oncology. He exudes professionalism.

Once, in the hall, he quietly remarked about my coming laparotomy: "Put a tape across your abdomen and write 'ouch' on it." In that minute, we were both ten years old, and I almost fell off the chair laughing.

March 3, 1976

I was scheduled for an 8 A.M. incision. I was up very early and watched the sun rise over the hills and city. I felt at rest. My mind once tried to elbow my peace to get its attention: "Can't you be a little nervous?" But somehow I was unshakable.

I was given a preoperative sedative. It made me feel like a little child trying to stay awake, not wanting to miss anything. Somehow the ceilings received this great attention as I was wheeled into the surgery room. The anaesthesiologist who ordered the ingredients of that haze was in the room. I told him, "I am remembering everything." Those were my last words.

I woke up in a body that was not sick, but tortured. I was in a room which seemed to contain lots of people stretched out in my state. It was as if we were on a battlefield of beds and some nurse in the distance was bending over to tend the injured and wounded soldiers. The face of Dr. Ed Temple, one of my surgeons, blurred in front of me. I just moaned for him as a dying soldier would do, and went back to sleep.

What a great capacity we have for pain. My first night, consciousness was nothing but torment. There was a tube down my nose reaching into my stomach, attached to a continuing suction machine that was not working properly and had to be replaced.

The call light in our room was broken. My roommate and I shared one hotel desk bell between us to ring for aid. Clara was in charge of it.

I could not talk or move my body. I could only grab a nurse's arm and pull her close to me and whisper, "I need more medication." She replied, "You just have to expect for it to hurt." I felt utterly dependent on others for survival.

In the morning Mike Mainer came, and I told him I needed a stronger dosage to counteract the pain. He understood. He said, "It was like going to hell and coming back." That was very profound, at the time.

Morphine was my consciousness-decreasing drug. For a while I had no awareness of the sequence of day and night. It was either dark or light when I opened my eyes. I had chest congestion and wanted to cough up a thick mucus, but it hurt too much. My body raged with fever in its own global warfare. I was taken on a stretcher for chest X rays.

After one injection of morphine I had a hallucination. A girl was weaving by my bed. She held out strands of colored yarn for me to see. She was gentle and I could see right through her.

I told the night nurse and she must have told a doctor on the floor. A very hip young medical man put his head around my yellow curtain and said, "Are you having a good trip?"

Somehow I began to mend in such small little ways, I could hardly tell. They helped me get up and walk. I felt like I was a tiny bug walking up the wall and across the ceiling. My world began to open to time and shifts and people.

When the doctors on family practice rounds came to see me after surgery, I had the overwhelming impression they were visiting a kitchen sink. Not only did I have a hose in my nose, but inserted in my wrist was a tube leading to a gravity-fed water bottle, and my urine was collected in a plastic bag.

Oh, humble kitchen sink, my porcelain was indeed chipped.

Friendships grow, and as they change, show their depth. Some are slow in the knowing and the growing, but last. With Dr. Cris Maranze, it was fast. We were always friends.

Cris was the family practice doctor who rotated into my surgery team after the operation.

She had very long hair. Mostly she had to twist it into rope and tie nautical knots to have a sanitary-code head.

She wore a white coat. One pocket bulged with mini prescription books of pills and dosages. The other held the tool that illuminated her hearing of inward processes.

At night she would come, and we would build ladders and attach extensions to them and climb up into ideas. In the morning she would come with the surgery glee team to ask if my bowels had moved yet.

One night she made a confidence. She introduced it by first swearing me to secrecy. I assured her I would never tell anyone and waited. She declared it was only in a best friend category that there could be such a disclosure. I waited. "My real name is Harriet and no one knows it." I never told anyone.

I told Cris how I could live on fifteen dollars a week for groceries. It was a life-style that made my mind as sharp as a stockbroker over the price trends of in-season produce. I was a merchant ship of store sales.

She wanted to know the stories of a lady at home, and I wanted to know the stories of a lady as a doctor.

Our respect was great toward each other.

I recovered into an air of comforting optimism about the findings from surgery. Everyone agreed as a group that it had looked and gone well. One of the team was a medical missionary candidate, and I nailed him alone to tell me the truth. He, too, agreed it looked good. A Christian family practice doctor confided that he had prayed for me outside the surgery door.

The staff member who dictated the operation record for my chart said under *Findings:* "The spleen was grossly normal," and the postoperative diagnosis was the same as the preoperative diagnosis: Stage II out of the four possible stages of Hodgkins.

I rested in the confidence of my doctors. On the morning of the pathology report, I remarked that the paper would be final that afternoon. The attending physician said, "That's right, but I don't expect them to find any abnormality."

Nothing prepared me to see such a grim Dr. Mainer come in and stand by the window, and such a serious Dr. Temple enter and lean against the wall.

"I have some bad news and good news," Mike Mainer said. "The spleen was enlarged, weighing 220 grams, involved with Hodgkin's disease, consistent with nodular sclerosing. The good news is I've talked with hematology, and you won't need any chemotherapy."

Mike talked as if he were reading a paper he had typed in his mind before coming in. They were very heavy words to have to say. He left the room. Dr. Temple stayed with me.

I was stunned. I knew I must be in Stage III. I could count my thoughts and emotions, as if my head had broken into a lot of little pieces and they were falling slow enough to number. I was mad at every encouraging word and that I had believed them.

We all stood two inches tall; I was set up for a fall. It was winter, and they took my only coat.

At that moment, I could see birds flying north again. They seemed free, and I felt bound.

I had studied Hodgkin's disease. Like an examination where the answers are on a page in your textbook, I could see the survival-rate graph for the third stage. The print was too small to read, but it was a reduced residue of years.

I have three little children, not even old enough for school.

That is so searing a thought, so like an AT WAR headline that I said it out loud.

Dr. Temple took some Kleenex out of the drawer and wiped my eyes. I hate to pull people into my drama: Let them be free. So I pulled out my defense mechanism, girded myself in its armor, snapped the visor over my eyes and asked, "How will this affect the managing treatment policy?"

Dr. Temple replied, "You will be scheduled for regular X rays and liver-spleen scans."

"But I don't even have a spleen any more."

"Oh, that's right," he said, softly, and left the room.

I was alone. What could I do with my mind? It was like I was in an elevator and my will could push the up or down button. I sang a portion from a song that a minor prophet sang thousands of years ago:

> Although the fig tree shall not blossom, neither shall fruit be in the vines; the labor of the olive shall fail, and the fields shall yield no meat; the flock shall be cut off from the fold, and there shall be no herd in the stalls; yet will I rejoice in the Lord, I will joy in the God of my salvation. The Lord, My God, is my strength (Habakkuk, 3:17, 18).

The song could be turned up and sung out loud, but I could not turn it off. It was like the Holy Ghost Radio Station.

My agony turned into a great joy that was beyond understanding: And joy is one with peace. I was in a very high place, and I wanted to look around. For a brief time I was on top of an embroidery, instead of on the bottom side where the knots are and the threads cross. It was a perfect work.

I wanted the doctors to come back so I could comfort them. But instead Clara came, and she knows how to weep with those that weep, and rejoice with those that rejoice.

I fell asleep making plans to go to Dr. Ritzman's Bible study in hospital South.

Tuesday, March 9, 1976

I could walk only with great discomfort. This was a little offset by bracing a pillow against my abdomen.

I got an extra-large pair of men's drawstring pajamas and inserted a feather pillow, firmly joining the strings as tightly as possible. I put a long maternity dress over this configuration, plumping and smoothing, looking full term. It was my only chance of being able to cross from hospital North to hospital South. I took a wheelchair, but abandoned it shortly thereafter.

I moved slowly through the early morning hall. The corridors were vacant until I saw a doctor whom I knew only slightly.

Dr. Haley looked at me and his face turned into vaguely funny shapes. Curiosity swung far beyond politeness, and he reached out his hand to touch my stomach. I drew back quickly and said, "Almost due." "Yes," he said, "almost due."

Later, I was told, he came into the clinic and asked, "Am I going crazy, or is Laurel Lee crazy? Didn't she just have her baby?"

I made it to the Bible study. When I returned to my room I felt like a great athlete.

With an abdominal incision, joy can be a real problem. It hurts very much to laugh. Sometimes I would just try to think of the most terrible things to sober a good humor, but my comic sense triumphed.

I had conflicts with some of the nursing staff. I would wait until I really needed pain medication before requesting it. Occasionally I asked a little earlier than the prescribed interval but always within a thirty-minute reef of the allowed time. They always refused, once stating I had a mere ten minutes before it could be allowed.

The rules are made for the patients; some nurses saw it that the patients are made for the rules.

I saw another thing, too. The registered nurses were often so busy maintaining IV bottles and pills that jobs were given to the aides that were beyond their capability or their sensitivity.

Perhaps my discomfort was producing intolerant observations. Our whole situation was exaggerated by having a single hotel bell with which to summon the staff.

At home Richard was involved in a pediatric thirty-two-hour rotation. Matthew and Anna both had the influenza. Thus I could not be discharged home, but a house opened up where I had never been before. I went from the hospital into this unknown hospitality.

The family have several children, and their pictures

took up two of the dining room walls. Most were grown now, and only two were left at home. I knew the mother had died of cancer last year, and I was sensitive to this grief.

They took me into a back bedroom, offering me books to read. The stack included a magazine called *Cancer Victims and Friends*. On the cover was a picture of shiny crystals of laetrile. Inside were reports about a Tijuana clinic and an underground railroad to transport those in need.

The books contrasted the nontoxic approach to cancer, through diet and natural supplements, with the toxic approach of radiation and surgery.

My body didn't feel well, and I had a stream of people coming to aid me in my transfer to the natural way. It was done out of true concern, yet it was over-whelming.

There were many voices urging me to consider my diet:

Your food shall be your medicine and your medicine shall be your food (Hippocrates, 424 B.C.).

BOOK A: Take nothing into your body that has been cooked or processed; if necessary sell the stove and buy a good juicer.
1. Give up meat immediately.
2. Give up milk in every form forever.

BOOK B: Only a pittance of the millions spent on cancer research has been used for nutritional investi-gation.
1. Experimental cancers develop most rapidly on low-protein diets.
2. I have yet to know a single adult to develop cancer who habitually drank a quart of milk a day.

Glasses of carrot juice (what's up doc?) and natural snacks were given to me.

My host took twenty-six pills with his dinner and confided that it was a lot less than at the beginning of his treatment. He opened his chest of drawers to share with me, and it was stuffed with bottles and bottles of natural supplements. "You are a junkie," I cried. Then my eye caught a white satin banner with the word *Mother* in gold lettering. It was from a funeral wreath.

I decided to chance the flu for the night and called Richard to come and take me home.

On one of my last nights in the hospital I had spoken to Richard on the phone. He told me he had been cleaning the closet.

When I was back home I found that he had taken a portion of my clothes and deposited them in a grocery-store lot Goodwill box. I shouted, "What do you think you are doing—getting rid of your dead wife's estate?"

"I thought about that," he answered.

I had lost my hand-knitted white sweater with red hearts on the shoulder. I'll find another cardigan, I argued back in my mind. It doesn't matter.

The next day, March 14

The clouds in the Portland sky were folded together. The children and I rode the airplane up through the mattresses and drab feather ticks we were bedded under, and there was the sun above Portland. We went to California for two weeks to stay with my parents, recover from surgery, and see the baby.

I was with all my children. I was so weak Matthew had to pull me in the big red wagon to the park. But I was with all my children again.

April 1976

I had a checkup in the hematology department. It was notorious for keeping patients waiting hours beyond their scheduled visits. I'm sure we got dusty we sat so long. "Cobwebs are growing between your back and the chair," I announced.

Collectively we had the impulse to clap when the nurse finally began to call for the patients.

The radiation field is set up with delicate precision. Behind one of the CAUTION: RADIATION signs is the simulator room, where the treatment area is calculated on a large machine with a Picker brand name. I was helped onto a table next to a panel of buttons. Arching over me was a hood, looking like a large green praying mantis, with dials of numbers for eyes. Its face was square, with lines called X and Y. There was a note which read, "Target to surface 40.3 centimeters."

The table centers its patient, and the lights are dimmed as the technicians take refuge in a lead-lined room of dials. Bells sound, and you can see your bones on a mounted TV screen.

These procedures are repeated with pieces of lead string marking certain spots, and then the boundaries are painted with flow pen. In this manner I was prepared for my next series of treatments.

I took the bus with the children for the first radiation on my abdomen. Returning home, I waited to transfer buses in the downtown city center. I felt altered but not sick.

An enormous red double-decker English bus, carrying advertisements for local stores, made its way down the street. The attached sign said FREE RIDE, with a map of the circle of stores it stops at.

Of course we all scrambled up its spiral stairs to sit on the tweedy plaid seats on the top. As we turned the corners, I began to feel a low level of nausea. The bus pulled into Import Plaza and parked as the driver blithely announced that this was the end of the line today.

I was beginning to feel very nauseated and a long way from home. "I'm sick, stay with me," convinced Matthew that the merry English bus ride was indeed over. I pulled the children with me through the run-down Burnside district. Matthew was excited at seeing all the empty bottles along the sidewalk. "Let's collect them and cash them in." I said, "There's no refund on wine bottles, Matthew."

We crossed by the casual labor office, and I knew I was going to need help. I tried to call a friend, but even the print was blurring in the phone book.

I began to vomit in a garbage can. A part of my mind could feel people driving by thinking: "Look at that . . . an alcoholic . . . at her age, and such little children . . ."

A social worker from the labor office came over to me. I said, "It's not what you think, it's radiation!" He was polite anyway and directed the children and me to our bus stop. I sat and leaned against the building, instructing Matthew to watch for the Number 40.

The ride was a long-suffering journey. I knew I was going to throw up again and decided that the most unobtrusive depository would be my purse.

I became a bus-ride attention center. I was passed one Kleenex, someone opened my window, and another moved as far from me as possible. The bus driver refused my transfer as I finally rang the bell two blocks beyond my stop. I climbed down the stairs and my purse spilled all over the sidewalk. That was the journey from Hiroshima to my bed.

The medications lessened the nausea; but I was always wading through it, and I could hardly eat. I said the word *food* backward. It was now *doof* and I didn't want any.

"I am going to turn into the bones that walk." The doctors had a solemn assembly: a staff member, my radiation resident, and two technicians. I joined them. They sat straight as arrows and first suggested reducing my dosage. Then they spoke again, "We feel you need marijuana." It was unreal. All of a sudden it was like a Peter Sellers movie, and we may as well all sing together "The ballad of the busted brownie . . ."

They stopped my expanding meditation by referring to an article from the *New England Journal of Medicine*. They told me about another young Hodgkin's patient who stated that he stayed stoned and well.

Cris Maranze pitched a copy of the article to me on her way to family practice clinic: "Antiemetic Effect of Delta-9-tetrahydrocannabinol in Patients Receiving Cancer Chemotherapy."

Dr. Moss began to take a new interest in my case. I gave him the article to read, and he personally administered the rad reduction. But he didn't feel that any "extra" medication was necessary.

As my strength decreased, an empathy grew in me for old people. I suffered from many of the common geriatric problems. I had to watch other people take over jobs that in health I could do with more efficiency.

One of the continents in my mind perceives not in words, but in shifting images. I felt like I was driving around in an old junk Studebaker body, where in health I was a four-wheel-drive jeep that climbed mountains.

I was sick. I was weak. I had fevers and weight loss. I was again admitted to the hospital.

HOSPITAL
MAY 10

There were no hospital beds for females available in hospital North, so I was sent to hospital South, where I had never camped. I was taken to the twelfth floor and assigned a bed next to a young girl in what looked like a body cast. She had her television going and sang along with all the commercial jingles as I changed into pajamas. She asked me if I liked Jesse James and showed me how far she could sit up, all in a matter of minutes.

I decided not to cross the sheets with my body and

Hospital, Hospital
Number Seven
Salvation is free
then there is Heaven

went to find a nurse in the hall. I asked for mercy. It was as if I'd been hitchhiking, and was picked up by a car with a crazy driver. They put me instead in a Cadillac: a large single room with a view. I rested in bed, so grateful, feeling as if I'd won the daytime TV prize. It was quiet.

Weakness is like being in another gravity zone where there is just not enough energy for activity. I had to plan my moves.

Pictures are like extra windows, and I had none. From the pediatric floor, I chose six different quilts and hung them on the wall and put them on my bed. I took plants from the lounge and put them on the window sill. I did all these things with the permission of the nursing staff. Then I rolled up my bed to enjoy the view.

The nurse brought me a note to sign. It read: "Consent to take full responsibility for bed to be in high position. The hospital is released from all responsibility for any accidents resulting."

There I lay all day, except for radiation.

The weekend schedule had reduced personnel and observation. My first Saturday back in the hospital, I made a secret arrangement with Stu Levy and Cris Maranze. I walked out to the main driveway between North and South and sat on the curb.

They were coming to get me for the afternoon. They pulled up in a junky white Chevrolet, the kind of car that looks like it was born at a drive-in movie.

Stu's hair hung down to the steering wheel. The tassel from his high school graduation cap (1966) hung down from the rear-view mirror.

Once Stu told me people could accept him as a craftsman or a farmer, but not as a medical doctor.

We went to the civic center. Stu went to an exhibit of photography equipment. Cris and I went to a funky junk show of neat old groovies.

I tired so fast, I could not last. I sat in a chair. Cris sat with me there.

I took out my embroidery thread and showed Cris how to make a herringbone stitch. She took off Stu's corduroy shirt and built a line of teepees in thread until we left.

Their house was in the hills by the Portland Rose Garden. On the step of their front porch was a foot scraper built out of two horseshoes.

In their library was a tree growing from a pot all the way to the ceiling. "That's Arthur the avocado," Stu explained.

Over the fireplace was a rock-'n'-roll band picture of the Sacred Mushroom boys. Stu's amplifiers stood like watchdog giants in the living room.

They showed slides of their Arizona backpacking trip.

Stu told me a special summer guest doctor was coming from New York. "Dr. Lipkin is a sage," said Stu. I visualized a Dr. Sage, who would look like he was from the Himalayas with long hair like Stu's, but solid white.

I fell asleep on their couch and they had to tiptoe around.

It's not me, it's just my body that acts like this.

I started to write my hospital journal, but I could only create a skeleton of experience with words.

Help is just somebody else's plan for you. I had a phone call from someone I did not know, who gave me the address of Dr. Contreras and his laetrile clinic in Mexico. A lady brought me two books advocating laetrile. They were too late. I was too tired to read them.

In the shower one morning I found more swollen lymph nodes in my groin. A biopsy was scheduled with Dr. Temple to determine if the malignancy had spread.

I talked to Richard and he spoke such a graphic phrase that I had to walk around it very slowly.

"Have you ever seen two dogs and one has been hit by a car," he said. "The other just walks around it and howls, not knowing what to do."

The night before the surgery I wanted to write. I went into a doctor's small office on the floor, because it had a desk and chair. A medical student was there, wearing a baroque parquet-floor tie and reading three books.

One was a jumble of crazy images, never coming to any conclusion, but nonetheless having power to play tag with the mind. It was called *Even Cowgirls Get the Blues*: "The brain that pound and a half of chicken-colored goo, so highly regarded (by the brain itself), to which is attributed intricate and mysterious powers, that slimy organ (it is the self-same brain that does the attributing). The brain is so weak that without its protective casing to support it, it simply collapses of its own weight. So it could not be a brain."

It's a new generation of doctors and mailmen, but the bankers always seem to remain the same.

Biopsy Day
Friday, May 21, 1976

It wasn't an early priority surgery, but it was to be done before noon. I decided the lymph enlargements were guilty of disease and had to be proven innocent. In this attitude I could have no letdown from pathology.

Only the pubic hair on the right side was removed, and I was given enough medication so that I would be relaxed during the incision procedure.

The first effect of the narcotic was that I began staring at a quilt that I had mounted at the foot of the bed, becoming wrapped in its design and color.

In this state of mind I was taken to the surgery floor, hospital South.

First I was wheeled behind a curtain, where one other girl was also waiting for her scheduled room and hour. Between us was a baby in a crib. The girl kept talking to the baby and would ask me or any passing nurse if we were the mother. I just thought she got more dope than I did. Then I was wheeled into surgery and transferred to the table. I was draped except for my face and entire groin area. Above Dr. Temple were two large lights that seemed like large bug's eyes, but not of a menacing species.

In this X-rated position, the staff surgeon walked in, looked at me, and asked Dr. Temple which side the biopsy was to be performed on.

Our minds can bring forth data in less than a second. I was immediately reminded of my first biopsy, when all the betadine preps were done on the left of my neck and without comment the node was removed from the right.

So I sat up on the table, looked at the staff surgeon and said, "The side where they shaved."

Then it was obvious that it was a dumb question. The nurses and doctors looked each other in the eyes, but the surgeon's position prevented us from laughing. It was one of those little moments common to all, where the emperor in the parade discovers he has no clothes on. We were the only two that had spoken, and without another word he left the operating room.

Dr. Temple made the incision. I could feel the blood run down my thigh.

Mike Mainer once shared in detail how a cesarean section is performed. I remembered all the steps and began to abstract. I allowed free play in my ideas and decided I was having a minute cesarean and was going to give birth to an infant the size of my thumbnail. I slept the rest of the afternoon.

A hematologist examined me. He had a closet of

pet lions, and his recommendations unleashed several for my contemplation. Their mouths were open.

"Although she is still, clinically, in Stage III, the severity of the symptoms makes more widespread involvement a possibility. Because of this, chemotherapy (MOPP) is in order. Normally, patient would be rested four to six weeks, completing radiation. However, because of the aggressiveness of the disease in this patient, that time may not be available. We are waiting staffs' opinion as to this.

"Suggest:

1. gallium scan
2. bone marrow
3. bone scan
4. liver scan
5. liver function test
6. surgical consultant for biopsy of inguinal mass"

These lions stayed in my room. At times they were very big, and I would tremble. Sometimes they were small, but they were always present, with teeth.

The biopsy report confirmed the spread of Hodgkin's. There were days to wait before Dr. Bagby and the staff returned from their convention. It was a time for me to consider the possibility of chemotherapy.

Dr. Ritzman sent a friend of his with fourth-stage Hodgkin's to my room. He said the only reason he was alive was chemotherapy.

But once Dr. Hood had said, "I've killed people with chemotherapy."

One text wrote, "Significantly, the sites of major toxicity of these chemotherapeutic agents are not all the same: Although most are myelotoxic, some primarily affect the nervous system or gastrointestinal tract" (*Cancer Journal for Clinicians*, December 1975).

Besides the concern of the cancer-causing agents, I did not want the top of my head to look like my knee. A disease and its treatment can be a series of humiliations, a chisel for humility.

My room had been an ice-skating rink. As I sat and wrote, I glided through the hours, leaped over barrels, and was exuberant.

Now there were holes I had to maneuver around. My feet could get wet and cold, and I would shiver on the bed.

I had an official pass for a weekend afternoon. I asked Richard if we could take a ride in the country. I was starved for landscape. I got dressed but he never came.

I felt like a sociology documentary I once saw of the unwed mother. Often she vests her expectations of security in a boyfriend who never comes to see her in the unwed mothers' home.

Later I reached him by telephone and he said he had taken Matthew, Anna, and some other children hiking.

The same weekend Mike Mainer asked me if I would like to go for a ride with him.

I asked Richard and he said it was a good idea.

Mike had a small German car with a window in the roof. We drove west through sloping farm fields. One meadow had a track of red flowers like a solid letter spelled into the earth.

"It's clover," I said.

"It's not clover," said Mike.

He backed up the car to settle the horticultural question. It was a crimson clover variety.

We waded out and I lay down in the scarlet verdure. It reminded me of when I was a child in Illinois and we would make imprints of angels in the fresh snow. We would wave our arms and legs into wings and dresses.

"Mike, there really is a Heaven," I said.

"I can't believe that," he answered.

"If we stood back in history three hundred years and I brought you a report of a continent I found with animals so different from those on your farm, you wouldn't have believed me then, either."

We ate tacos in a drive-in. We went back to the hospital. I shared with him one square of my worry about Richard's attitude toward me.

"Stay as close to him as you can," Mike told me.

Friends arranged to bring my children for a few hours. I was so excited. I went up to the pediatric floor and walked past the wall mural of Snow White into the game room. I explained to the volunteer that I wanted to borrow some toys and I would bring them back. I filled a red wagon with mechanical wonders, stories, and dolls. I took the stars and left the cast of thousands.

I got a bowl of crushed ice and little bags of a crunchy kind of food.

The children came; ever moving, ever talking bursts of energy. They had a style of appearing to explode into an infinity of perceiving parts. We flowed together.

When they left I was so exhausted I could hardly move or speak. I wanted to remove the toys. A sadness permeated my being. Maybe all the storybooks had sad endings. I hit the wrong floor button and wandered around, a stranger pulling a crazy wagon in her nightgown.

As I slept a nurse took the cloth wrapping off a sterile instrument. He smoothed out the material. He painted with a blue flow pen a moon face with wide eyes and an enormous crescent smile.

He climbed over my bed. He climbed over my plants and hung this banner down from my window, using the extra-wide masking tape.

It was the first thing I saw in the morning.

The day came when some of the hematologist's six recommended points would stick me. They were planning to do a bone marrow. I waited.

The hematology staff chief had returned; he came into my room with Dr. Bagby and Mike Mainer. He said he was not convinced that chemotherapy or any of the tests were at all necessary. The inguinal nodes were an untreated radiation port, thus their enlargement did not mean I had had a relapse. His recommendation was a discharge from the hospital, with a further course of radiation on an outpatient basis.

He took every lion with him. I roared for joy. I wanted to tear up that first hematologist. As Mike Mainer left the room, he told me to "Love thy neighbor as thyself," and closed the door.

On my very last day, a man came and introduced himself as the technician who once gave me a barium swallow. "Look," he said, "these are the stains on my pants when you spit out the drink."

LOVE THY NEIGHBOR AS THYSELF

I took down the quilts, put the plants back and went home.

Thursday, May 27

Home is said to be the one place you can go and they have to take you in. If I'm a rock thrown in the water, home is one of the first rings from the weight. It is you in things.

I walked into someone else's house at my old-shoe address.

The living room was not the grandmother lace card where I once read *David Copperfield*. Now there was a television set against the wall.

I had only allowed the kitchen counter a line of antique cans. Now there was a beach of practical kitchen movement: A silver toaster had its electric-cord hand under a blender umbrella; an electric can opener was wearing a green plastic bikini; tacky vendor stands of canisters advertised "flour" and "sugar."

"This is how it's going to stay. I couldn't find anything," said Richard. "And that stove," indicating my blue enamel queen on her ornate throne, "has to go. It makes the pans black."

So I walked through the house and the floors were slanted uphill.

Friday, May 28

Richard took the children to the baby-sitter.

Saturday

He helped the baby-sitter take her dirty clothes to the laundromat. She was a young girl raising two children alone and her car didn't work.

Sunday

> This was the day my house fell down.
> Remember it brown,
> Like the ground.

I always operated under ordinances. I was allowed Sunday school and that was my formal religious training time boundary. The children went to their classes and I sat in the back, listening to adult admonitions.

The pastor's wife asked if I would stay and share from the pulpit in the main service. It was like a new application of working out my salvation with fear and trembling. An elder escorted me to the platform after the congregation sang:

Storm clouds will come
Strong winds will blow,
But I've got a Savior
And He's sweet I know.

The faces spread out before me. There was a television camera for the auxiliary room. It's a large congregation.

I made paragraphs. I left the rostrum. I left my Bible. I left the church. I was tired.

Richard took the children hiking. It was raining and they were wrapped in blue nylon zip suits. His last words were, "The fire will go out in three hours."

The pastor's wife came by with my old ragged-flag Bible. She brought me a new one with large print and references. The elders had signed it. I paraphrased their message to "keep on trucking."

Richard never came home. It was night. *If I were a mouse in a cold old house, what a cold old mouse I would be.*

I called the baby-sitter. They were there. They had all gone hiking together.

Thoughts flew around in my head. I understood that to him I was dead.

We talked that night. "We're in two different kingdoms," he said.

How can two walk together unless they be agreed? The feeling of love that promotes tap-dancing down supermarket aisles, leaping over bushes, catching blooms between the toes; that goes. But the fact of love becomes a code of behavior.

"Love suffers long, and is kind, seeks not its own, is not easily provoked." But there is only rest when every eye stays in the nest.

As I put the children to bed late that night, they leaned out of their bunks built from plate glass packing crates to sing. They had Sunday school songs. They pounded their fists one on top of the other and the lyrics ran:

> The wise man built his house upon the rock
> And the house on the rock stood firm.
> The storm came up,
> And the rain came down,
> And the house on the rock stood firm.
> The foolish man built his house upon the sand
> The storm came up,
> And the rain came down
> And the house on the sand went squish . . .

They spread out their fingers and sang it again.

Monday, Memorial Day

Friends opened houses to me. Richard started to file
for divorce.

The Wade family was a cloud of dew in my summer
heat. I had my radiation series to slug out and I slid
each night into their home plate. They gave me their
bed, and they slept on the couch. The Wades had two
little girls. I watched the family well and long; they
were sound.

I ached in concern for my children. They came to
visit me. It was a comfort that youth could be so in-
sulated by their merry hearts.

I was in the wilderness of my life. I was a Gretel
without a Hansel lost in the woods. There was a wicked

witch who would eat me if I would listen. *In my thoughts were my wars fought.*

> Weeping may endure for the night,
> But joy cometh in the morning (Psalms 30:5).

I rented the upstairs of an old house. I turned each window into a greenhouse. The children came home. Anna played Maple Leaf, a child's interpretation of the words *make believe*. There was no more outbreak of Hodgkin's disease among the doll family. The dolls only had colds.

I finished my journal. I was shy to show it, but I gave it to Mike Mainer. From him it passed in and out of the residents' mailboxes.

I had my last radiation treatment. I was young again. I had completed all the medical course possible unless the disease recurred.

In Oregon, the salmon run from the sea to their

spawning ground. There are nets. There are sporting men. There are rocks and ascents so steep some die from the journey itself. But some silver salmon make it home. It's a matter of percentage; it always is. I could grow old.

My last treatment was the very day family practice clinic had a farewell dinner for its graduating residents. We ate on the roof in the sunshine.

Stu could only grab a hasty plate, as he still had tables up and down the hall to serve, like a Dr. Waiter.

I pretended that I was graduating, too.

The head of family practice put his arms straight out to the side and said, "I'm an airplane."

"I'm a cloud," I said, and he hugged me.

I met another guest in the hall, Stu's sage, Dr. Mack Lipkin from New York.

After that day Stu called and organized a videotape session with Mack Lipkin and myself.

Dr. Lipkin came into the studio reading my book. He had his thumb on the page where the breast pump looked like a bicycle horn.

Stu cared more about our comfort than the clarity of the recorded picture. He dimmed the major illuminating lamps to reduce the heat.

I had borrowed a copy of Mack Lipkin's book. He's an authority in his field, and has served as a consultant to the Surgeon General. I shared one of my favorite paragraphs, where Dr. Lipkin was speaking with the head of a major medical center. He told him that he thinks it should be required that every graduating doctor first produce a bowel movement in a horizontal position with three witnesses present.

"Is that right?" asked Stu.

"Yes," said Dr. Lipkin.

Dr. Lipkin asked me to come to his office the following Monday at nine in the morning.

After an eclipse, the sun emerges from the shadow.

One morning a man from church came to my door and offered me a scholarship to Bible school.

Friends contributed to buy me a round-trip airplane ticket. It was a vacation in a box addressed "to Mexico for Laurel." The children were to go to their grandparents' house while I traveled south.

Monday, July 26, 1976

I had to hurry to make my appointment. I rushed out into the early morning street and waited for my bus.

An antique store had been closed for a long time. This was the day they were loading the furniture into a large rented truck.

"Oh," I sighed, knowing I should wait for the bus, but I entered the shop. The owner sold me a wooden cuckoo clock for a quarter. I turned its face into my dress so it looked like I was only carrying a large birdhouse.

The owner went and stood on the curb, overseeing the hoisting of his furniture pieces.

I saw the orange bus at the top of the hill. "Look, I didn't miss it at all."

The proprietor emerged again and gave a gift to me. It was a rich leather book called *Blessed Be God.* The pictures were in such hairline detail they could be printed into religious paper money.

I entered Dr. Lipkin's office on the third floor of the family practice building.

He said he found some charm in my book and asked to send it to an editor friend in New York.

I felt like I was a very homely girl who someone thought could be in a beauty contest.

I jumped up and down in my chair and somehow this activated the clock in my lap. It went "Cuckoo, cuckoo" over and over until I thought I was flying over the cuckoo's nest.

What could I give Mack Lipkin, wise sage, great doctor? I had a little sketchbook of watercolors I had made of passages in Thoreau's *Walden*. I ripped out a favorite page: "The essential laws of man's existence do not change just as our bones are indistinguishable from those of our ancestors."

My book went to New York. It was like a piece of paper a child floats out into a stream. It was soon out of sight. It will get caught in some weeds, I thought. There are holes in it. It will fill with water and sink.

But I lifted up and flew on.

SIGNS OF SPRING

For the friends of Henry Robbins
with love

If the writers of the world took chairs in an orchestra pit, each would hold the instrument that he plays best. There are first- and second-string fiction writers; biographers are at the oboe; historians play the cello; poets are the flutists. Somewhere in the symphony are those who love a journal.

SIGNS OF SPRING

At the age of seven I started my first journal, using a pastepot to secure on the page pictures cut from magazines. The visual aids were the troops to back up my small vocabulary on the front line. I wanted to capture all my thoughts and adventures and keep them safe within the diary. As I grew up, I continued to record my life's outward events as well as my inward reflections. In the evolution of the journals, I made small watercolors and drawings as windows in my text.

In October 1975 I started a record of a very special voyage. I found myself suffering unusual symptoms while caring for my two children, and pregnant with a third. Tests at the University of Oregon Medical School in Portland showed I had a form of cancer. It was diagnosed as Hodgkin's disease, a malignancy infecting the lymph node system.

The medical staff recommended a therapeutic abortion before beginning radiation therapy. At that time, in the seventh month of my pregnancy, I refused to abort. As the tumors continued to enlarge, aggressive radiation treatment was started at the risk of damage to the child.

A healthy daughter, Mary Elisabeth, was born, but I continued to have surgery and X-ray therapy as the disease progressed into its final stages. Considering the situations, I wrote in my journal:

> The disease gathers at an unseen degree
> as poisoned brooks become rivers
> and rivers run into the sea.

My husband faced the possibility of raising three very young children alone. After witnessing my seven hospitalizations, which covered a period of almost nine months, he found himself unable to cope any further with the circumstances. He moved out of the house and filed for a divorce.

At the end of July 1976 I was given an unexpected gift: the attending physicians pronounced the therapy successful. The doctors explained that it was not a cure but an abating of the disease into the state they called "remission." All clinically visible evidence of Hodgkin's disease was gone. I felt like Noah in the new world after the flood. Every continent in my life had been rearranged.

The journal of my hospital stay had not been written with publication in mind, yet a visiting doctor, Mack Lipkin, insisted on sending it off to publishing friends in New York. I then began another diary as I faced my new life, raising my three children alone in the strange new state of remission, a place I'd never visited before.

August 1976

The Willamette River divides Portland East and West. I rented the upstairs of a house on the East side, seventy-six blocks from the water. It was an urban camping site, and the rent was prorated to a three-dollar-a-day fee.

I had to make a place for three children to sleep within the two small rooms of the apartment. I folded a sleeping bag to equal the two-board width of the closet shelf, and this mattress construction was covered with a sheet. I taped mountain photographs on the inside of the door and boosted Matthew to the altitude of his rock-shelf bedroom. He had a flashlight, and it was a six-year-old adventurer's life. The baby's cot was staked in the living room closet. Anna slept with me, but I didn't sleep just with Anna. She was an animal keeper, and we lay with her stuffed wild beasts.

Reaching into our porch mailbox, I pulled out a post-card with a glossy layout of free gifts for saving depositors and an envelope from the city courthouse.

I unfolded a form letter stating that our marriage was dissolved. I had not signed my name, seen a lawyer, or gone to court, yet I discovered that I was legally divorced.

The "in sickness and in health" clause had dried and faded. For better or for worse, my husband had blown away. I looked up into the leaves and thought of how they keep their promise to the tree, abiding on the branch through gusts and storms.

August 5

Everybody has a neighbor. Hazel Wittenberg lived across the street. I could count on her for tea and advice, and her backyard for Matthew when I had a doctor's appointment.

Age four can be a performer that doesn't see the

audience beyond the act. Anna sang in her seat on the bus, a two-line rhyming ditty. As her mother, I looked for adult eyes to affirm that she was cute. No one returned my glance.

The girls watched their feet tap a reflection on the hospital corridor linoleum. Looking into the waiting rooms of different departments, I thought of the frequency of medical checkups for any patient either advanced in a pregnancy or stricken with fatal disease. It must be a physician's "welcome wagon service" for those coming and going.

In the radiation therapy office I gave Anna magazines and Mary Elisabeth a page to tear into small ragged pieces. I was ushered into the examining room across from the betatron equipment. The machine vibrated through the closed door.

Dr. Anderson was entirely in white except for a red film clip on his lapel to gauge his own X-ray exposure.

He reminded me that the Hodgkin's disease had progressed below my diaphragm, infiltrating the spleen before remission was effected by total nodal radiation.

His introduction gave him time to draw his guns. He shot straight at me.

"With most Hodgkin's patients in your stage and cell-type category, remissions are usually not long-lasting.

A relapse, where the disease returns, could occur within two years."

He projected my abbreviated life expectancy without feeling. I wanted to cry. His lack of compassion either in pause or phrase made me feel that he was on the side of statistics and against me. I decided to receive the prognosis as coldly as he gave it. My throat ached from holding back a cry. We were at war and his gun had yet another round.

"We saturated the tumor with aggressive dosages of radiation. In killing the cancer cells there has been considerable aging to your organs and skeletal structure."

Under the fire of his words I retreated. A standard rose in my mind. I remembered Moses. Though he lived 120 years, his own natural strength had not faded. I did not know if I stood on a manifestation of hope or faith, but I smiled back at Dr. Anderson.

August 9

I knew I would never receive a check for child support. I remembered my old procedure for supplementing the minimal income of a school bus driver. I still had the hand-lettered sign that read GARAGE SALE. It was my grown-up Kool-Aid stand to provide for extras beyond rent and utilities. I had been mother "playing store" for small change.

I kept putting off the call to the Welfare office. When it became a matter of our pending hunger, I slammed the refrigerator door shut, grabbed the telephone book, and looked up Multnomah County help.

The public assistance waiting room was full of women with small children. On a rack, next to government-issued pamphlets on nutrition, were magazines. I picked up a three-year-old copy of *Family Circle* and thought of every place I know with periodicals available to the public for reading. I saw that a facility could be ranked in terms of magazine dates. Airplanes and private doctors have current subscriptions. The donated reading material in clinics has a six months' lag. At the bottom of the list was the Welfare office: every ragged issue was over a year old.

The receptionist gave me a lengthy questionnaire to determine my eligibility. I filled it out with a pen that was chained to the table. I spelled out the names and birth dates of my dependent children. It was an inverted application form providing blanks for the listing of scars, not stars. Personal references were required to support the statements of genuine lack.

When the check came with the food stamp voucher, I carried the papers upstairs. As my left foot hit the stairs, I said, "Crisis situation," and the right foot pounded back, "But not a life-style."

August 14

Cancer was the word that walked on padded feet and stalked me. At night, as I lay measuring the children's breaths, it pounced on me. The claws were the doctor's warning of relapse.

I ran my hand across my chest looking for symptoms of recurrence in a night sweat. Finding no perspiration, my care could evaporate.

I rose to a factory of raising children to be healthy and wise. I punched in at dawn with a bottle of milk for Mary Elisabeth. I tightened the daily bolts of whole wheat toast to the table.

I knew I was going to have to talk to the children about their father's absence. Not knowing how to do it, I waited.

Anna came in from summer play and watched me put my kitchen shelves in order. She asked me if Daddy was just waiting for the house to be cleaned before coming home.

"I'll answer that at lunch," I said. "Go get your brother." I was in a countdown for time. I didn't want to injure their idea of their father, but yet wanted to let them know he wouldn't be living with us.

I leaned against the counter watching the children from the perspective of their youth and vulnerability. Mary Elisabeth lifted the high-chair tray and dropped it to watch her bread crust jump. Matthew was rotating his sandwich in his hand, trying to turn the square bread into a wheel by controlled bites.

I took a breath and said, "Your father loves you very much, even though he has gone to live at another's house." I thought if we could see this sentence in the air, it would arc like an expression of grief over us.

Anna had only one thing to say: "I had hoped he would choose us." I chased her statement with three bowls, filling each one with too much ice cream.

I took them to the park and pushed them on the swings higher and harder than I ever had before.

August 15

Matthew found a scrap pile of irregular lumber. He laid a cross board over a middle plank. "Wings," he said. Smaller pieces were laced front and back. He came to me asking for the tools to shorten and secure a propeller and tail. Hammer and nails were life to him. I opened empty hands in reply.

His disappointed look registered his realization of the cost of being the only male in the family. I couldn't enter the wonder kingdom of construction.

The children asked to see their father. There's a need beyond food and sleep.

I called him at his friend's house. Divorce is the death of communication; our sentences contained only the hour of his visit. He wanted them waiting for him by the curb.

To them, Richard had legs like a giant. He stood above every daddy. He knew the number of stars and the constellations by name.

Once alone, I thought that, in every madness, the home was the regret.

August 17

As the baby slept and the children played outside, I thought about my ten-year gap in relationships with men. I had been perfecting, in small moments, the quality of closet shelves and matching-sock drawer arrangements.

I resented being forced back in time to once again think about single men. I could see that the need for companionship was going to make me reach out, even if I dragged my feet at the thought of doing it.

I stood announcing "The Available Man Fire Drill." In a hasty, loud way, I ran through my apartment proclaiming my interests and talents.

"See those quilts"—indicating my sewing basket. "It's nothing for me to piece together original patterns! And that jam," I said, moving into the kitchen. "It's all home-made."

I heard Matthew coming up the stairs. "And here he comes," I was shouting now. "My favorite single man!" It wasn't my son after all, but a friend from church. He gave me a look of genuine concern.

August 20

Thunder and lightning were married and had such a fight in the night that they woke up the neighborhood. Mary Elisabeth stood crying in her crib. Matthew requested aid. I took them into the comfort station of my bed.

I could not sleep at the press of elbows at my side. There was no distraction in the dark, no small chore to occupy my attention. I wondered at God about my circumstance.

Before words come pictures, and I saw a vessel on a potter's wheel. The sides of the clay were being pinched to create lines into its form. Pressure improved it. The way of surviving is to find meaning in suffering.

August 25

I kept wondering about the fate of my hospital journal. I was concerned that Dr. Lipkin's friends had misplaced it. It had disappeared in the East Coast mystery of publication submission. I decided to be a sleuth of the missing manuscript. I would write a bloodhound letter, revealing "I did it"; looking for the clue "Who has it?"

I didn't have any stationery, only art paper. I tried to cut it down to correspondence size. My scissors kept making a stack of irregular imperfects, always sawing one leg shorter. In frustration, I folded the page in half, with the choice of cutting an ear that would open into a heart, or half a pine tree. I chose the woods and wrote:

Dear Editor:

I feel like the country mouse writing the city mouse a letter. . . .

I continued my laps around the track of raising children. I missed passing the evening baton for the final sprint of bath and pajamas. Without a teammate, there's loneliness in the long-distance run.

I longed for an adult to talk to. My conversation was limited to instructing three underdeveloped countries. I had to stop them when they yelled at each other before they escalated into small-arms combat.

I became a telephone junkie in my craving for mature conversation. Starting with small calls, I increased my daily intake.

I ignored the danger signs of abuse. I began to like the dial tone. There was a euphoric feeling that my night had begun only when I heard a responding grown-up speak into the receiver. One evening the only mature voice I could reach was the metallic recording of the time.

I went into the bathroom and looked into the mirror. I traced with my eyes the three lines in my forehead, and then looked directly into the pupils.

"I think you are going crazy."

"Yes," I replied, "this proves it."

"I don't think we have ever just sat down and talked like this before."

Then I could think of nothing more to say to myself. I had to pray. Prayers can range from sighs directed upward, to essays written to a Quaker God, "Thou alone art worthy." The inside of me, sitting on the vanity, spoke. The outside reflected my need. Seeing one tear, I said, "See." But not to myself.

I concluded, free for a joke. "What is the definition of a home permanent?" "A woman with little children," I quipped back. "Now I'll stop shaving my legs and pronounce them in a state of mourning."

Hazel Wittenberg came over to pause from her duty of sorting dark and light clothes for wash. She had on her working uniform of polyester knit pants. She talked while running a finger over some threads that had pulled loose on her knee. She told me of her husband's willing hand to help in chores.

I felt a dart enter my heart as I heard her speak about his considerateness. I built a wall of literature, ducked behind it, and threw a rock at her. I quoted the first line of a book: "Happy families are all alike, unhappy ones are different each in their own way."

I found only a snare in measuring and comparing myself with others. I had to sort my dark and light thoughts. I didn't want to make a Kleenex box my centerpiece.

I was in a desert. I thought of my parents' house surrounded by palm trees. I called and my mother offered me water. I made reservations to go south for two weeks. It would be the oasis of a middle passage; a space between two life-styles.

a parents house
has a required costume
sometime seams
can be so constraining
that they pinch
walking and talking

Fremont, California, August 29

A peculiar chemistry takes place at the door of my parents' house. Somehow, between turning the simulated brass doorknob and stepping onto the beige carpet, my molecules lose their structure. I stand in need of their reconstruction.

The children only needed to be fed. My mother first exclaimed that they were growing; she didn't have to bend over as far for their hug. She then led them from the entrance hall to her refrigerator. There was a box of Popsicles waiting.

After dinner, the television is a kind of night clock. It has programs for numbers, and the screen is the dial.

I left my parents behind their portable snack trays. My father said good night, reaching into his jar of pressure-packed peanuts. The children were already asleep. The dishwasher light drew a shadow from my feet as I walked through the kitchen to my room.

I sat on the bed swinging my feet. The problem of supporting three children weighed on me. Poverty and disease towered over me. With all three at home, I wanted to be there with them. No one could put on a Band-Aid as I could.

My apartment was too small to take in other children to baby-sit as an "at home" employment. I didn't know how to iron. I needed to offer an unusual craft or home service. I thought of learning taxidermy so I could stuff Columbia River salmon for fishermen. I could mount the small game on the kitchen table.

Or, on supermarket bulletin boards, I could publicize a letter-writing service. I could specialize in penning direct mail to relatives, and offer a budget line of postcards.

I thought the most dishonest thing would be to consider marriage as a means of support. I wasn't ready for another union. Those who refinance by taking a husband work the hardest for their income, and have sorrow with it.

I faced giants in the land. I couldn't control my circumstance, only my reaction. I jumped to my feet shouting, *"No one can be a David without a Goliath."*

I fell asleep thinking of submitting an original line of watercolor designs to the manufacturers of Kleenex boxes. There could be two series, one issue for those with colds, and another for those in grief.

Berkeley, September 1

I wanted to take Matthew to Berkeley and show him the Victorian residence where he was born. The station for the rapid transit system is so modern that Matthew thought it had fallen from the sky.

Designed to use a minimum of public employees, it has no agents selling tickets, just machines. The equipment collected our fare, simultaneously showing the increasing sum on a lit panel as I deposited the coins. I needed my years of experience using candy bar vending boxes to transport us to Berkeley.

We walked to the house, following Strawberry Creek at the pace of a child finding rocks and leaves. There was a man dancing very slowly in the eucalyptus grove.

"What a funny act," said Matthew.

We went over the bank and up onto the Plaza by Sather Gate.

On the stairs was a man wrapped in a shimmering bedspread with a red velvet collar. A monocle was held by a string, he had spats and a muslin head wrap. He carried a cardboard sign that read: ASK THE MAN THAT KNOWS PAST, PRESENT, AND FUTURE.

A crowd gathered as he hit a brass plate to announce himself as the wizard of Berkeley. Matthew took our lunch and darted away, not wanting to see him.

The wizard began: "My art is practiced by witch doctors in Africa, priests in ancient Egypt, and great wizards of all generations."

A skeptical volunteer was asked to write the name of a deceased person in an occult symbol. The wizard ripped the paper into little pieces, dropped it in a can, and soaked it in lighter fluid. He asked for someone to help him light it. One man, with a long braid, was reclining on the stairs, and cried out, "I only know how to set bombs."

The wizard described the pictures crossing his mind. Finishing his imagery, he announced the name "Nikolai" to the crowd. The volunteer confirmed his answer.

I found Matthew feeding the birds with grains of salt-sized bread crumbs, and explained to him:

*There shall not be found among you . . . a witch
. . . or a consulter with familiar spirits, or a wizard.
. . . For all that do these things are an abomination
unto the Lord.*

(DEUTERONOMY)

One backpacker, at an intersection on Telegraph Avenue, had on big earphones from a high-fidelity set. As he passed us, he exposed one ear and said, "I'm listening to nothing." "He's saying nothing, too," said Matthew.

I saw the turrets of the landmark home and pointed out our old room above the sandal makers' shop. I told Matthew his first bed had been a handmade crib hung by rope from the ceiling. Below our window, a car used to be parked, inscribed "THE STONED AGE" in eight-inch caps.

I remembered coming to Berkeley, leaving an isolated rent-free cabin, to have the baby. We moved into a small backyard pup tent in the last trimester of my pregnancy.

I had walked through the streets hoping someone had left a rent-free house in an abandoned paper sack or on a bus stop bench. I found it while crossing at an intersection, when a man had offered my husband and myself a manager's job.

The house, appearing to be condemned, provided the cheapest rent in Berkeley. We were the superintendents, overseeing seven rooms that shared two baths and a kitchen.

Memory ranges from the recording of facts without emotion to the recollection of feelings that obscure every detail. I could remember the joy of putting the tent in its stuff bag and standing up at night in a warm room. A concept of immortality is with the young: in those days, I thought I would never be sick.

Matthew rang the bell (they had improved the security system in the past six years). To my amazement, the mysterious Mr. Knolls answered our ring. He had resided under our management, slipping in and out of his room, avoiding all human contact. No one ever saw the inside of his domain: he had spray-painted his one window. His teeth had all rotted away or broken off in the front. All the places in his clothing that had received the most wear, like elbows and knees, were bare.

He invited us into his room. As I pushed against the door he said, "You probably won't be able to open it." Matthew said, "I can." He always rises to a challenge of strength.

Before I could voice my reluctance, Matthew had

managed to squeeze through a crack in the door. I followed him into a room that was a nest of newspapers. One pile towered above our heads. There was a great paper wall around a single mattress littered with clothes. Matthew stared and said nothing.

On our return trip to Fremont, Matthew asked about all the strange people he had seen. I paraphrased a truth for him: "Many who promise liberty are themselves the servants of corruption."

September 5

My mother sat across from me drinking coffee. The interiors of some of her cups have a haze from their years of service. I watched her cigarette smoke as an almost invisible host moving between us. She told me a lot of people in the family have had cancer, but I was the first one to be divorced.

A visit with parents is like a ball dropped to bounce in place. The momentum of greeting is its height. It loses altitude after the news is shared, and hardly clears the floor in admonitions.

Portland, September 7

The suitcase lay open on the floor like a square figure eight. The contents of it doubled with the clothes my mother had purchased for her grandchildren in clearance sales.

Back home with the children, California faded from my mind. Double-knit shorts and tops were my only proof that it had existed. It seemed a dream, where I crossed from sleep into waking with things. Again, I opened my distribution service of Band-Aids.

Over a cup of tea, Hazel encouraged me to lean on God as my husband. She opened a Bible on a wooden stand and read:

> For the Lord hath called thee as a woman forsaken and grieved in spirit, and a wife of youth, when thou wast refused. . . . With great mercies will I gather thee.
>
> (ISAIAH)

She suggested that I join the singles' group at church.

I was cautious of any singles' marketplace. Those once married increasingly take more shelf space. There can be dents in their tin from previous handling.

I got a call from Andrew Rodell. I had known of him in the congregation for years. He had a side business in bee husbandry and managed an automotive shop that boasted a sign exposed to the freeway:

POWER TO THE PEOPLE'S CAR
PEACE IT TOGETHER
VOLKSWAGEN.

He asked us to ride with him to deliver a bee colony that a farmer had rented: we were to pick it up at a storage lot and deliver it to a field. I pictured Andrew in my mind. All his sentences had to find passage first through a tangle of red beard, then into the receiver.

The children curled on top of sleeping bags as we

drove west of city center. Andrew turned his face for an instant from the steering wheel and looked me full in the face.

"Working with bees is something a family can do together."

I dropped my eyes to his shirt collar. A small row of embroidered cross-stitches was started on one side.

Andrew sealed the lid to hoist the colony into the back of the van. He knocked it against the bumper, wrenching it apart at one of the flats. The air was full of the droning of bees.

He pulled the children out by their feet and I ran with them down the dirt road. We were all stung and the children cried.

I expected an apology, but none was offered. Instead, he had a cheerful explanation:

"It's hard to work with bees and not be stung. There's enough money in it, though, to support a family."

We returned to Portland.

After saying good night, I shepherded the children upstairs. I was thinking: when one commits oneself to a marriage, it's not only to a man, but also to a way of life. I sang out loud, "It ain't me, babe. No, no, no, it ain't me you're lookin' for."

"Now," said Anna. "Why would I be looking for you when you're right here?"

September 11

I registered Matthew in a first grade class a block from our apartment. A nondenominational school called Temple Christian, it required a dress code of blue shirts for the boys. I had to take all three children with me when shopping for Matthew's school clothes. It was Sherman's march to the sea, walking to the bus. It was Hannibal crossing the Alps as they scrambled to different seats for their ride to Eighty-second Avenue.

Value Village advertises itself as a nonprofit thrift store. The donated goods are divided into bins and racks. The racks are more expensive, separately priced garments on hangers. I went to the bins, large tables heaped with clothes categorized by size or function. At the shirt table, I chose three appropriate cotton classics for a quarter apiece. I found a canvas lunch sack riveted with leather handles. One side was stenciled: "Good Equipment Makes Better Farmers."

A parent's whole perception changes toward the child who forsakes crawling to walk erect. The mother takes a deep breath and the time it takes to exhale is no longer than the phrase: "They're growing up!" It was the same for me watching my eldest leave for his first day of school.

I went to Hazel's to talk about it. She gave me the look of "Oh, come on. That's three-minus-one more freedom."

September 20

Matthew hid his canvas sack behind the chest of drawers. Everyone else, he explained, had a glossy tin lunch box. He was feeling the pain of being different. I still had enough funds from the September welfare check to allow him to choose a simulated school bus from a display shelf. I hoped, in his first rush of peer pressure, he assumed it was common among his classmates to sleep on a closet shelf.

October 3

The Portland skies are often overcast. The city is the gray lady of the Columbia River. While cutting out newspaper food coupons, I received a telephone call from a literary agent announcing the sale of my journal to a publisher. The news folded back the dark roof of the sky. My financial captivity had been turned. My tongue filled with singing and my mouth was full of laughter.

I could not stay in one place with my news. I gave the little girls to Hazel and ran down the street to Matthew's grammar school. I calmed myself enough to walk to his desk in a "Here, you forgot your lunch" kind of stride. I whispered to him about the publication. He was the first to register the news as a personal demand. Bowing his head slightly, he said, "Now I'll have to learn how to read."

The editor called the same afternoon. I had called my journal *Laurel Lee Goes to the Hospital*. He wanted to change the name and call it *Walking Through the Fire*. I was conscious that we were talking long distance and at the high daytime rate. In consideration, I began to speak fast, bumping my sentences into each other without pause. He told me to enlarge the book by elaborating on my account, and asked me to bring the new material to New York within the month.

I couldn't tell if I were on top of a mountain, or in a hole. The excitement was up, but the pressure was down.

Every intent to write was interrupted by the children. Matthew developed a series of stories that had to be bound into his own book. Still too young to print words, he dictated them to me every evening. I was his faithful recorder:

This is a true story. This version is very true and I am Mommy's son. Now, let's go on with the story now. When I was in bed, angels appeared on my ceiling. It was so bright, I thought they were wasting electricity. . . .

I discovered that ideas don't know what time it is. They woke me up at night. They insisted I follow their logic at dawn. So that the night light wouldn't wake the house, I closed the bathroom door and balanced with my pen on the laundry pile.

In preparation for my trip, I called a mother of one of Matthew's classmates. Ida Hamilton said that she would be glad to take the children into her home. She was the kind of woman who was born with a sewing machine under her arm. I explained it would only be for one week.

October 12

Hazel was going to take me to the airport. She asked if I could take some apples to a relative in New York. The morning of my flight, she brought over half a case of local apples.

I took everything out of my suitcase, filled the bottom half, and still had more to pack. I packed my purse; it could not be fastened together with a mound of fruit between the handles. I watched it go through the X-ray machine at the airport: one fruit cellar handbag full of bombs. I thought to myself, "I can't arrive in New York like this! My agent and my editor are going to meet me. They will think that I am Johnny Appleseed." At last I sat down and began to remove apples from my bag. So occupied, I missed my nonstop flight east and had to take the next one, where I would have to transfer planes in Chicago.

I turned to the seat behind me and found the technician who had operated the first radiation machine used in my treatment. Then I walked up the aisle and found three doctors from the radiation department. They were all going to an oncology convention. None of us knew that the others were on the flight. Every time the stewardess came up the aisle, I was sitting with a different man.

"My, you are a friendly person," she remarked.

In all the excitement I couldn't eat. My years with little had created a depression-living consciousness; I couldn't waste food, so I wrapped the "friendly sky" sandwich for later.

I got off the plane and no one was there to greet me. I just sat in my red corduroy suit with its missing button, covered by a belt, and went over survival theorems. "When lost in the woods, stay in one place."

A man in a turtleneck sweater approached me. He was Henry, my editor. We hooked together like train cars going down the same track and took our position with Harriet, my newfound agent. We were the New York Express.

We went to Harriet's apartment, where I was going to stay. It had a glass observatory looking into the New York skyline. She pointed and announced the Empire State Building. Somehow, I confused my landmarks and created an image of the Statue of Liberty. I began to peer out, looking for a metal lady with an arm up in the air. "I don't see it." Both Harriet and Henry began to gesture into the skyline. The truth dawned on me and I wanted to make amends.

"Oh yes! The Empire State Building. That's what Hong Kong climbed."

"King Kong," Henry corrected me gently.

We all went out to dinner. To an anthropologist, no one is without culture. I had stumbled into a society of amiable restaurant dwellers.

October 13

The receptionist in the publishing house lobby smoked a thin cigar. She inhaled first, releasing the smoke as she queried my business. The more she planned to say, the more intensely she sucked on the lit tobacco as a preliminary for speech. Above her were display shelves of books. I was overwhelmed with the feeling that I was visiting a refined horse-racing establishment. Each title had left the stall and was meticulously clocked for its speed in producing winnings.

In a glass display case was the original Winnie-the-Pooh. He was receiving an honorary wreath for having made laps for the past fifty years.

My editor was expecting me. Henry was the doctor to the newborn manuscript. He checked the pulse of the pages as a vital sign; the letter can kill, but the spirit gives life. I signed the birth certificate of a contract.

A good editor works on the posturing of sentences. He makes them hold back their shoulders and sit up straight. He makes paragraphs walk in a straight line.

In Oregon, I have seen the Tillamook cheese factory and have been on a tour of the salmon cannery. I had the feeling I was on a field trip the whole day.

I found an apartment's yard surrounded by a wrought-iron fence. A tree grew out of a plot the size of a throw rug. From its lower branch hung a hand-lettered sign: "If Anyone Should See a Tree Vandal, Please Call the Police." Even the garbage cans were chained to the fence. I was staring at everything.

I had never known businesswomen. The ladies of my life knew casserole recipes. Harriet knew what time it was around the world. She owned a lot of jewelry. While others have Kodak photos to remember occasions and people, Harriet has neck loops and bracelets.

One of the friends of the literary agency holds the office of treasurer to the United Nations. He invited Harriet and me for lunch in the delegates' dining room. He was to meet us at the visitors' entrance.

We left Harriet's office late because she had received an overseas phone call. The taxi crawled through the yellow paste of city cabs down to the East River. I was anxious about being late, so I ran ahead to meet the treasurer and apologize about our tardiness. I rushed into my story, outlining our delays. But then I realized that the man listening to my account was dressed in the ornate coat of the door guards. Behind him was standing the treasurer and I exclaimed:

"Oh, you would never have to wear a uniform, unless it had all the coins of the world sewn on it!"

There are so many delegates, beyond the dining room's seating capacity, that lunch reservations are very strict. We had lost our seats some time ago and had to follow the waiter from table to table.

"The United Kingdom had reserved this table. Can you be finished by one o'clock?"

"Impossible," replied our host.

So we went to the next table, and in this manner made our way around the entire dining room. It seemed like a musical. I expected Third World powers to dance, and we were poised at the edge of a song.

I regarded the buildings of New York as a fisherman might eye the waves of the sea. Its force claimed cargoes, and multitudes had drowned; whereas my voyage was calm and my nets full.

Harriet invited her friends to what she called a "cocktail party" my last night in the city. Everyone remained standing and talking in knots of two or three. I kept contrasting the social occasion with equivalent gatherings of "Christian fellowship" where we sit and sing.

I went into the kitchen. Harriet's refrigerator had modern single-women food:

1 glass jar of raspberries from England
2 bottles of Champagne
1 can of almond-flavored macaroons
1 glass jar of marinara sauce
an assortment of preserves
an imported gold-foil tin of English pudding
a United Airlines napkin, wrapped around my old sandwich

I heard the word "Hodgkin's" through the louvered door. A doctor who knew about my case was talking to my editor.

"Confidentially, she may not live to see it in print, Henry. Her remission may not be long-lasting. With the aggression of fourth-stage involvement, I would recommend rushing publication."

I had been floating in a bubble of observation. The sphere had colors flowing through its film. It was pricked by the doctor's concern for my remission. I felt the weight of being back on my feet and carrying the load of fragile health.

Portland, October 22

I woke up, and in the instant between waking and the opening of my eyes, I couldn't remember where I was. I made it a game. For that second in the dark, I had to remember. I was home again.

The house of a parent is a child-care center with the best facilities, including a backyard for the summer and a basement for the winter. The cold weather brought everyone into a shrinking living room.

My need for quiet was great inspiration to create games to keep the children on the stairwell:

The child on the top stair is Noah. He names an animal. The child on the bottom begins to climb the gangplank into the Ark, imitating all the characteristics of the beast called. Reaching the top, he becomes the new Noah and the other returns to the bottom tread, only to slither, hop, or roar back up. . . .

Anna went to answer the door buzzer, and brought Andrew Rodell up to our apartment. He gave me a quart of honey and set his felt hat with a Tyrolean ribbon on a chair. He asked me if I was taking natural vitamins, offering to order some for me at distributor price. He read *Prevention* magazine and shared a quote from an article:

> *As one tree creates a particular fruit, so does the cancer-prone body create malignant cells.*

I played dumb and made sport by offering him a natural-energy snack. "I use extra-soft white bread spread with real butter and sugar."

I paid for my jest. Matthew and Anna were transported by the idea of such a sweet food and kept asking for it all afternoon.

A FOR SALE sign, shaped like a bell, was planted by the porch of the house across the street. I asked the price, and heard an amount possible for me to afford because of my income from the sale of the book. The residing family, the Millers, had lived there for twenty years. The realtor explained to me that the date of their move was contingent upon the house that they were to buy. I followed through with all the serious business of house-buying, then led the children in a parade through the new backyard and around the apple tree. Mary Elisabeth's portable stroller was our only float.

November

I was so anxious to move that I imagined, as I opened my closet, that I was shaking hands with the doorknob to say good-bye! We would have bedrooms for each one of us.

My glimpse of a two-story floor plan exaggerated the smallness of our quarters. I felt I was Alice in Wonderland swollen to an enormous state. Wanting to sleep alone, I put Anna in the bathtub with a sleeping bag for the night. Matthew climbed up to his shelf. I opened Mary Elisabeth's closet door. Her Port-A-Crib touched all four walls.

I counted the quiet. Alone in bed, I enumerated the silence. Before reaching number 6, the baby threw her bottle into the living room. At number 8 Matthew said he was too hot. By number 12 Anna crawled into bed with me. The cast-iron tub was too hard for her. I quoted for myself the lines by Lewis Carroll:

> *'Twas brillig, and the slithy toves*
> *Did gyre and gimble in the wabe.*

November 15

Acquaintances are always stopping me with the question "How are you doing?" Knowing that I am in remission, their queries have a certain edge as well as polite salutation. Once having walked with the inescapable company of death, the pulse of my health is checked all the time, in the expectation that one season my strength will fail. So the question within me is "How long will I be doing well?"

I kept my scheduled appointments at the radiation department. The waiting room had the same quality of silence as passengers in an elevator. I could see Dr. Anderson in the hall recording the weight of an emaciated man standing on a scale.

During the examination, I divided my attention between the doctor and a painting of old-fashioned girls in blooming dresses in a garden. Dr. Anderson said he could find no evidence of disease. He asked me if I would go and visit a young woman with bone cancer. We took the stairs instead of the elevator.

He turned to inform me, "Her name is Kathy, she is twenty-six and very ill." I expanded the list, adding the word "terminal."

He left us alone. She was fading into the pillow. Four inches of hair had grown out since chemotherapy, giving her an elfin look. Beyond identification, I felt as though I were looking into my own face. There's a sphere in weakness when even speech takes effort. We hardly had strength for words. I was stricken by her youth and her dying. It was Kathy herself who was troubled on every side, but not distressed. She was perplexed, but not in despair: cast down, but not destroyed. Even though her outward frame was perishing, her spirit was renewed each day.

I left wondering why Dr. Anderson had brought me to visit her. I didn't know who was to comfort whom.

December

Our refrigerator door was a continuous gallery of young art. The first winter reflection came in a purple-dot snowstorm. Matthew brought in his new Christmas tree picture from his first grade class, which looked like it was hovering over a skyline of high-rise presents.

It began to look as though we were not to have Christmas in the new house, but in our little stable. I could only think of Mary's accommodations; she gave birth in a barn.

There is a time line to Christmas. My first Noel deadline was Christmas cards. The exchange of them was my special winter garden. They were cast out like seeds in white envelopes and I harvested their return in my mailbox. Some hang their yield on the wall in rows.

December 16

The act of bringing in the Christmas tree was our centerfold in preparing for the holiday. I wrap ornaments in the grocery ads to see the price rise of a year. Decorating the tree is a matter of perception. Anna and Matthew were exclusively garnishing the branch that was level with their necks. I tried to encourage them to conceive of the tree as a whole. Yet only their fronds received thorough and complete attention. Anna rolled tissues and attached them to the tree by forcing the needles through a strategically bitten hole. I thought it gave the tree an overpowering effect of suffering from a bad cold.

Matthew had a number of pictures from school. His vision was to mount them at the three-foot level. Mary

Elisabeth could crawl and reach, so the very bottom was absolutely bare. She spent the season delighted with the water in the red metal stand.

I popped popcorn and gave Matthew and Anna a needle and thread. They added four-inch popcorn strings and I explained that our final touch would be tinsel. "It's to look like ice drips."

So, with the sound of a great howling wind, Matthew threw the tinsel, because he knew ice formations could only come in a storm. Anna joined him like a blue norther, and we were finished.

I store presents. I am a squirrel with a good nut and I bury them under my bed. Garage sales are my floating bazaar, and little children don't care if a toy is second-hand. *It's not that I am poor, it's just that I don't have any money.*

While I was embroidering a blouse for a gift, the telephone rang with the news that the Millers were finally going to move on Saturday.

December 18

It was a cold morning as the Millers and their friends carried their belongings out to a pickup truck. We ran to get boxes from the grocery store. We never crossed the street again with our hands empty. Once they were stacked, I balanced cartons on the stroller handle. Matthew carried his, Anna carried hers, and we looked like three box turtles going home.

Andrew brought his van to help move the heavier furniture. From his army fatigue jacket he produced vitamin C tablets the size of a quarter to swallow at random. He had a bag of almonds in another pocket. I read the label of a Bend, Oregon, health food store on the cellophane wrap. He explained that he had gone there to negotiate some property where he could keep his bees and remodel the garage on the lot into a home.

As we carried my treadle machine down the stairs, I posed a question to him with a multiple-choice answer.

What was his idea of a nice way to spend an evening?
  a. In a wood-working project?
  b. A long and quiet dinner?
  c. Visiting a remote and foreign village?

His answer was to build something. Behind us, Anna was carrying my sewing basket. She asked what I would pick. To my reply of a foreign village, Anna elected for herself a whole evening of bread, butter, and sugar sandwiches.

The Millers had taken all the light bulbs with them. I had one floor light for a bedroom. The house was without form, dark and wild. The children and I put our sleeping gear by the Port-A-Crib and spent another night with all our blankets touching.

By Christmas we were each in our own rooms.

January 1977

Our house looked as if it had been in a number of street fights. The paint was scratched. The garage had no door, giving the impression that its front tooth had been knocked out. But life in our new home meant I could escape living in merely one room with the family. With affection, I stenciled Pennsylvania Dutch hearts on the backs of the treads going upstairs.

February

Richard called, asking to see Matthew and Anna for the afternoon. Because of his short and simple sentences, I felt he was reading the request from a primary grade textbook. As usual, he wanted them outside waiting by the curb.

Beside me, Mary Elisabeth pulled herself to her feet on the cupboard door. She batted the telephone cord as I talked. She tasted it. She sang a song to it. The coils were alive to her hand.

When the children rushed outside, I zipped Mary Elisabeth into her snowsuit. At five weeks, she had gone to live with my parents because of my lengthy hospitalizations. When she returned to be with our family, Richard had already moved out. Mary Elisabeth had had her first birthday last month. I lifted her up to the car window so her father could see how much she had grown.

Richard grimaced at our sight. His friend sat next to him in the car. She was pregnant, and her size strained her winter coat. One gloved hand held the swell of her stomach.

A fist pushed my heart against a grater. I walked back inside with tiny hurting pieces loose within me. The baby sobbed in my arms because she had such a short time in the cold. I sat with her in the rocking chair.

A personal offense is like a scratch on a phonograph record. I couldn't move my thoughts beyond my pain. It kept repeating, as if I were stuck within its grooves. There was only one way to play beyond it. I had to forgive them, so my heart could take its form again.

There seem to be embers to divorce; slow-burning coals of memory that ignite in dreams.

Richard and I were together again in the texture of my sleep. We were the sole managers of a Los Angeles elephant retirement farm. Behind the recreation room was an old chicken section which needed our help.

The weight of raising three children alone collapsed through the canopy of my dreams.

February 21

I went to two other departments in the hospital, where I had checkups as well as radiation therapy. The hemotology clinic met on Tuesday afternoons in hospital North. Many of the people in the waiting room were coming in weekly to receive chemotherapy. In an adjacent office, a social worker explained to a patient the financial aid programs. To those who qualified, it helped offset the high cost of the therapy drugs. Sometimes I could see the nurse pushing the IV stand down the hall between the examining rooms.

Cris Maranze was my physician in the family practice

clinic. She told me cross-country skiing stories and summer camping plans. The doctors in each department were participating in the same search for recurring malignancy in swollen lymph nodes.

I felt I had taken one step off home plate with a bat. I did not strike out in any of the three departments' examinations. I hit a home run. I hummed on the Glisan Street bus a phrase from a childhood baseball song, "And I don't care if I ever come back. . . ."

Once home, I pulled a picture postcard of Mount Hood out of my mailbox. Andrew Rodell wrote that he had moved to Bend and was looking for a storefront to rent. He wanted to sell honey and wood stoves, and stock a line of vitamins. I hoped he would find his wealth and health.

March 5

I was the circus master of the morning. I had to beckon the wild boy from his bed and tame him for school. There was the fine high-wire acrobatics of keeping his sisters asleep, keeping our act in only one ring. I was in the stance of the juggler, crossing the lunch box sandwiches with the breakfast toast, when the telephone rang.

It was my editor from New York; Harriet was on the party line also, and they had news for me. It was the real Big Top calling; the Barnum & Bailey of New York. Henry told me to sit down, to listen. My book had been sold to a paperback house for an almost unbelievable amount. Half would go to my publisher and half to me in staggered payments. The connection began to crackle: there was bacon frying in the wires. New York said they would call me right back. I turned from the receiver and said to my son, "God has just given us lots of dollars!"

"But will we have any cents?" Matthew asked.

When Matthew had left for school, I sat alone and considered my fortune. A children's story came to my mind of a pilgrim walking up a narrow path. Above him, the sun and the wind each boasted of their strength. They waged a contest, challenging the other to remove the journeyman's cape. The wind tried first, but in the force of its blasts the man wrapped himself tighter in his covering. Then the sun took his turn, and the intensity of the illumination caused the cape to be flung off.

I thought of how I was like that man whose covering was godly faith. In the storm of difficulty, I held the old truths closely. But there is challenge in the heat of success. I bowed myself down on the floor. There was a new responsibility.

The first thing that I did with my expanded income was to leave the heat on all night. I had three children and had never had a washing machine. Dirty laundry used to reproduce itself into an overpopulation crisis. I used to build scale models of the mountains of the world next to the bathtub. From the showroom of appliances, I first bought a washing machine and then put a dryer in my basement.

I used to practice "faith-drawer opening." Not having done the wash, and needing clothes for the children, I would stand in front of their chest and remember the multiplying of loaves and fishes. I had needed the same manifestation for T-shirts and underwear.

I had never driven a car. The thought of using two feet and both hands to run a machine astounded me. I had only used tools that required one hand for operation. I stood on the fringe of the mechanical age.

The divorce had moved me and the children from the passenger seat of an automobile to the city bus system. I kept a set of bus schedules in every purse. Twice an hour, I could go to city center. I calculated all local distances in terms of the number of transfers necessary to reach my destination. Matthew and Anna took turns jumbling the coins into the fare box.

The desire to drive started with the one-syllable thought of a car. A new mobility was a hammer on my fears, pounding a path to a dealership which offered models with good gas mileage. When I signed the title, I encouraged myself to think of the children and me on a picnic miles from any bus route. By making such an enormous purchase, I would be forced to master the art of driving. Matthew was elated by the mini station wagon in our driveway. He explained he had been wanting a place to put bumper stickers.

I took chalk and drew an uppercase *G* on my pants legs as a visual aid in coordinating the right foot for the gas pedal. I put a *B* on the left leg for the brake. They became the first letters Mary Elisabeth could identify. I was an on-the-road "Sesame Street."

Hazel gave me hours of instruction in parking lots and on back roads. I learned not to close my eyes when caught in the terror of intersections. It finally seemed possible that I wouldn't need a summer bus pass after all.

I drove an hour away from Portland for my licensing examination. The Department of Motor Vehicles was empty and the examiner was near the age of retirement. He put on his jacket embossed with state seals and checked my turn signals, brake lights, and horn. The office was on a street that intersected the main avenue. It was the one hour of traffic congestion. I waited for a break in the traffic. My nervous emotion altered time. I felt the elderly examiner was spending his last days with me, holding the score sheet. I decided that unless I did something, we would never emerge. I stepped on the gas and squeaked between two cars. I lost thirty-six points in my first maneuver.

I sought other people who had also failed in their first attempt, and asked them to share their experience: "How I was first defeated, but later conquered it all." I saw the license as an ultimate award of skill. I practiced and waited to try again.

April

Molly, an apartment house neighbor, from Kotzebue, Alaska, explained that she could move in with us as a house helper until the summer. She told stories of seal hunts and feeding dry fish to sled dogs. She knew over one hundred words for "snow."

As goods increase, so do the mouths of those that eat them.

My towels resembled the covering of a target from firing arm practice. There were small holes among the tufts of terry cloth. Some had a fringe that originated from constant use, not the manufacturer's design. For the first time, I could replace them with new ones from a department store.

After making my purchase, I sought refuge from the multitude of displays in the store snack counter. The stools were arranged in a horseshoe for space and expediency. Neon light panels cast an onstage illumination. Every seat was occupied with ladies having lunch. The script on all the shopping bags should have read: "The Eye of Man Is Never Full," instead of the store slogan, "Like It, Buy It."

There were elderly women wearing coats with scatter pins. Some still wore small rhinestone Christmas trees on their lapels. Young women used crackers to quiet their children, redeeming time for coffee. Girls, sharing the same beauty concept as their friends, sat together looking like each other. The whole aging process could be traced in the faces.

All flesh is as grass, I kept thinking. It withers and fades away. I decided to make an appointment to draw up a will. In life or death, the children were my responsibility.

April 11

My legal counselor labored under framed pictures of eight successive generations of family lawyers. I sat watching the black and white eyes of all his relatives.

Family pride
Can be cold
And dearly bought.
Bones of ancestors,
First thing taught
And last to rot.

I wanted legal paragraphs like Christmas socks that would equally provide for the three children. He made a return appointment for the signing of my will.

April 12

I went back to the lawyer's office. He had managed to work my simple requests into six pages of the solemn language of the courts: a binding document requiring witnesses to my signature. Other lawyers from the firm stood behind me as I was asked to initial my consent to the pages.

In those seconds of making two capital *L*'s at the bottom of the page, I knew that when this is read again, I will be gone. Dying is a grief, but not death. I began to sing "When the Roll Is Called Up Yonder, I'll Be There." After the last page, I turned around and half of the lawyers were blushing.

April 20

Matthew was about to go outside. He had strewn plastic snap-together construction pieces across the rug. I asked him again to pick up his Lego blocks. My words fell from my mouth, lay lifeless on the floor, and disappeared through the kitchen linoleum. I refired my sentence, raising my voice to propel it farther, and tied a threat to the landing gear. Matthew pantomimed being wounded at the front door. With some thrashing from the injury, he turned back to do his chore.

The fine seam of discipline had unraveled. Not having a father at home was the loss of a supporting voice to any of my commands. Gone was the final word spoken in such a tone of authority that the children hastened to obey.

At times I'm in a squad car with a revolving colored light. I'm the judge deciding what is a misdemeanor or a felony. I stand in the ultimate execution chamber, getting my yardstick down from the kitchen doorframe. May the rod and reproof give wisdom.

The yardstick was a gift from the garage Andrew Rodell used to manage. Stamped above the numbers was the phrase SERVICE TO ALL SMALL ENGINES.

May

I felt a change come spring. Anna thought Mother Nature was God's wife. She spoke of the force that moves whales and pushes birds north.

With publication, the windows of our life would open and people would look in at us.

I often sat on the front porch staring into the flower beds. At night, I would awake suddenly and watch the black room turn into the dark forms of furniture. I thought continually on the effect of public exposure: I feared it would strike another blow to our family life.

An archer in public relations sent arrows of impending instructions. I was going to be shot into the target of the media.

The wind would whistle in my ears.

I took the children out to eat one evening. Anna turned the menu until it stood up, resembling a tent.

"Hey," she shouted at Matthew. "My hand is camping." She held her fingers upright and walked them into the tent, flopping them on their side so they could sleep. Matthew inverted the remaining menus, mincing his fingers like Anna's.

"We need rivers," he added.

In an instant, a spoon went into the drinking glass and was used to make wet streaks around the campground. With one sentence, I brought them back to a city restaurant and their dinner.

In my purse was the letter from my publisher. I had been thinking about it all day.

To the public eye, a waitress takes the customer's order and serves the food. But there's additional labor in her auxiliary work: filling salt shakers and cleaning the hot-chocolate machine.

I learned that a writer is required for more than just serving paragraphs. There are chores behind the counter. I would have to go on national tours to promote the sale of the book.

But I couldn't take the children, and would have to

leave them with the Hamiltons.

Mary Elisabeth was using her elbow to push a water spot across the high-chair tray. "Go," she said. It was her favorite word. Matthew and Anna were thrilled. They wanted to go to their friends' house.

"Mr. Hamilton has a garage full of tools and fixes old cars," said Matthew.

Their enthusiasm gave me confidence that my feet would be turning in the right direction.

Sometimes what is good is the enemy of what is perfect

May 28

My publisher's advertising director came to Portland. Lois was to fly with me for the first part of my promotion tour. I had told her stories from my past. I shared how my life had drastically changed from those earlier years of making my home in a basement and having residence in a chicken coop. Once I had rented a Berkeley storage closet for my dwelling place. Some children wanted it for their clubhouse after my vacancy. I hitchhiked to Alaska with only seventy-five dollars. . . .

Lois interrupted my storytelling for me to get my suitcase before leaving for the airport. It was already packed and in the car. Instead, I picked up a black plastic garbage bag with the food I was leaving for my neighbor. Lois stared at what she thought to be my luggage. I laughed, spilled the milk, and had a wet sock for the flight.

While on tour, I was booked to stay in large hotels. Most of the guests were attending conventions, which I had never known about. It's a phenomenon of business life hidden from people like myself who vacation in campgrounds. I met the insurance women of America in San Francisco. They wore polyester pantsuits and their business seemed to be the election of the next year's convention site. In San Diego, I was the only guest who was not a son of Italy.

June 13

In Dallas, the hotel had a convention hall welcoming the National Cemetery Association. There were booths for the display items. As I walked between the rows, the suppliers of the graveyard industry showed wares that increased the profit of death. One man at a display table thrust a pamphlet into my hand. The cover read: "Earn millions of dollars selling the original slumber bed vault."

There were ovens that reduced corpses to ashes in one and one-half hours. I saw the original twin-packed crematorium, advertised to meet funeral pollution standards. There were shelves of urns for the remains, even some built like books. A tractor corporation had a grave-digging device to set the coffin down in the earth. Every corner of the exhibit hall had a bar. I went back to my room.

I felt that Hodgkin's disease was a hound pursuing me. From the doctor's first warning of relapse, I knew it was on my trail. It was baying under cancer patients' beds when I visited the hospital ward. I have seen its shadow in the chemotherapy clinic. At this convention, its prints were everywhere.

I know what is behind me. I know what is before me. How small are those continuums of time and space compared to what can lie within.

Airplanes became my sitting room. Boarding gates were my front door. I could hardly enter an aircraft without remembering my Berkeley roommate. Once, she crossed the plane's threshold in her bare feet. The pilot turned to her and said, "You'll have to get a pair of shoes." She walked away dumbfounded. She thought he had said, "You'll have to get a parachute."

New York, June 17

Appearing on a national television show creates feelings of terror. Before, I was only in danger of choking locally. Now I could self-destruct 3,500 miles wide. I could be the living twenty thousand leaks under the sea.

Lois came with me to the studio. We were ushered into a green waiting room and sat with the secretary and a television transmitting the program. The Gideons should add that room to their list of places they leave their free Bibles. I was afraid.

I was brought out into the lights. I just had to remember not to mix cancer with another disease, as I had once done:

"While I was six months pregnant, they discovered that I had leprosy. . . ."

June 18

I had an appointment with a television producer. When the elevator released me to the specified floor, I walked out into a waiting room that was designed by a mind that loved space stations. The walls, devoid of pictures, were composed of a texture reminiscent of petrified cottage cheese. The starkness was intersected, but not relieved, by a runner of aluminum foil making a silver jet stream through the enclosure. A young lady who sat at a marble crescent verified my appointment.

The producer came in, and I was struck by the sight of his electric white hair and feet. His shoe leather seemed to be cut from a beast that was still in flight. He spoke with authority.

"It really is a miracle what has happened to you."

A miracle is an exception to statistics, or an exceptional statistic.

His plan was to make a two-hour television film. He said that the scriptwriter was presently in Los Angeles with an associate producer. He outlined a schedule whereby the company would pay my expenses to fly to Beverly Hills to meet with them for one day. Then, I would be returned to Portland.

June 19

I was exhausted by my schedule. I had been in media communications where existence had no more depth than

53

the shaking of hands with a microphone and living in a receiving line.

I wanted to make a friendly overture to the man who was to be my flight partner for the next five hours over the United States. Seeing that he had an Italian name band, I thought making a little joke would break the ice.

"I bet you belong to the Mafia: being an Italian and flying first class."

In Oregon, it would have been humorous, but not on a flight originating in New York. The chill factor of his look froze my eyes one hundred and eighty degrees from his face. I looked out the window.

"Sir," I said. "Even people in the Mafia have a front job. What do you do?"

"I install air conditioners," he replied.

I looked at his hands, and they were covered with rings. He then asked me about my employment. "Right now, I'm doing a film consultation on a book I wrote." It was a relief not to mention my long career as a part-time waitress.

I was given an hour's rest before joining the script-writer and the producer at Studio City. It was an hour of misgivings.

Books seem to be nothing but a diving board to film makers. They leap off the platform, unable to fall straight into the water. Instead, a twist of a one and one-half gainer is added to the plot. I didn't want a cannonball or a jackknife.

One portable bar was kept in the CBS executive secretary's office in a filing cabinet under the listing of "priority business." I was given a glass of French mineral water while everyone else had a drink. The executive office was spacious. The executive was spacious. He wore tennis shoes and a sweat shirt.

There was a sign on the wall:

The making of a movie is like a stagecoach ride. At first, you hope for a pleasant journey, but by the end, you just want to get there.

(TRUFFAUT)

June 21

On my way home, an older man with a young couple boarded the plane in Los Angeles. With some chagrin, they had to wait to be in flight before they could drink. Then they moved from seat to seat, introducing themselves and turning the first class section into a cocktail party.

I spoke with the woman in the group. She was a director of television commercials, traveling to Portland to pick up one of the private planes of the eldest in their party. "He is a multimillionaire," she explained. My imagination named him "Mr. Bucks."

I was watching the coastline out the window when "Mr. Bucks" himself came to ask me a favor. He wrapped a one-hundred-dollar bill in an address, requesting me to mail a book to him. I refused, for I'm not a mailing service, and stated that the measure of a man is not what he owns. We landed in Portland.

The woman producer offered me a lift home en route to their hotel. They had a limousine service waiting for them. An elongated silver Cadillac, flanked by a chauffeur in a black cap, stirred the youngsters on Seventy-sixth Street, all the way to my lawn. My little children wouldn't be back until the following day because they had gone on an outing with the Hamiltons.

Mr. Bucks got out of the car, taking another hundred-dollar bill out of his pocket and sent the driver out for refreshments. He played a game of Frisbee. The young woman sat on the grass reading, and the young man asked if he could make a credit-card call to his restaurant chain. I wondered how I had gotten into all of this, and why I couldn't just bring home lost dogs like everyone else.

Mr. Bucks came to me with either sweat or tears in his eyes. "There's meaning in giving," he said and then outlined a plan to take all the neighborhood children for a ride in his private plane. He had a pilot on call. We flew over Mount Hood and our own neighborhood.

I am learning, here a little, there a little,
line upon line, precept upon precept.

June 22

I resumed the repair of broken and lost shoes. I clocked more mileage in rocking-chair hugs and again opened my distribution service of Band-Aids.

I made the children's favorite pancakes.

From a bowl of batter
To a mound on the platter;
In the middle
Of the skillet
A sizzling splatter.

We ate spies, as I shaped the batter into dark glasses and a mustache for each of us.

We went outside to put in a small but late garden. I had six tomato plants to press into the earth. Anna was jumbling radish seeds along a row.

There is no warmth without some clouds, nor an overcast sky without some light. They asked me for their dad: they wanted him to come home.

"When does the divorce end?" asked Matthew as he spaded the ground. I posed a question and answered it myself:

"What can happen to a chain when it's pulled hard from both ends? It can come apart at a link. I was so sick that he decided to marry a helper so that he wouldn't have to take care of you three alone."

Anna knew a solution. "If Daddy got a new mother, you could marry a new father." She suggested the man who worked in the Montavilla Park Summer Craft Program. My laugh came from my mouth and not my heart.

I put the children to sleep that night like an airline flight attendant. After serving them water, I buckled their blankets around them. I was thankful their night's flight was in separate bedrooms.

I thought about remarriage. There would be few strong enough to cross the moat of my situation, especially if I ever again became ill. I cannot spend my days looking for a knight.

June 23

I studied the car in the driveway from my window. It

reminded me of a washing machine on a rural southern porch. Never used, it's visibly placed as a symbol of prosperity. I determined to finally get my license.

I chose a suburban state vehicle office at a morning midpoint. There was an influx of people from new housing developments making the examination by appointment only. We were told to come back later in the day.

I left the children in the waiting room with Hazel. Walking to the car, I paused to flash a victory sign at Matthew and Anna through the window. I left a number on the dashboard, according to the directions, and waited for my instructor.

Growing bored staring at a cement block wall, I reclined in my seat. A woman wearing a red hat with a state seal on it got in the car on the passenger's side. Still in a horizontal position, I asked her if she thought they would ever design cars with an elaborate mirror system allowing drivers to rest while in motion. "No," she said. Thin strands of saliva connected her upper and lower lips.

Entering a one-way street, I turned into the wrong lane. Once back in the parking lot, the examiner was showing me my low score when the children rushed out to the car. Learning I had flunked again, Matthew remarked that Daddy would always pass.

I rode home in silence. I took the examination failure as the sum at the bottom of the problems in my life. Feeling sorry for myself, I put a box in my mind and invited self-pity to stand on it and address me. When given the floor, he had a loud and convincing oratory. I was moved to tears. There is warfare in attitude.

Over the phone that night, a friend outlined a documentary film about a mentally handicapped person's struggle and success at getting a driver's license.

"We all have different talents," I replied.

June 27

Any household request for Matthew's labor brought a variety of negative responses. I called them his National Park System of saying no. He had an old-bear growl for Yellowstone. The Rockies were a stony silence with a chip on his shoulder. He bristled for California Redwoods. I was one girl ranger in the wilderness of raising a son.

I regarded his reactions as a series of distress responses. I left the girls with a baby-sitter to take Matthew for a walk in the evening. We watched our shadows in the streetlight stretch from our feet and shrink back under our shoes. I kicked a rock on the sidewalk, and the sport of keeping it in motion between us was born. I told a three-minute story about catching summer fireflies in Illinois when I was seven. Then I asked what was bothering him.

His answer was like water. I had to wade through the shallows of his complaints about Anna, to the depths of having only girls in his life. When we returned to the porch steps, he asked me to find a man to be his friend.

I sat at the telephone. Matthew's father was busy in the care of an infant and two other children from his wife's first marriage. He couldn't help.

I called Matthew's grandfather in California and outlined my son's request for a man.

"He needs someone who likes erector sets and Swiss army knives."

My father suggested making reservations for his grandson to fly to California later in August. The promise of a camping trip was made over the phone. Matthew wanted to shake on it, so he pumped the cord up and down, saying good-bye.

I went to bed imagining a silk-screen pattern to stencil on the children's clothes. The front would read: "Religion that is pure is . . ." The back would conclude: ". . . visiting fatherless children in their affliction."

July 3

I kept my summer appointment at the radiation department.

There was a line of wooden chairs with ashtrays in the hall by the receptionist. Cancer doesn't cure smoking. An enormous NO SMOKING sign was hung in the waiting room. Dr. Anderson motioned me to come in. He was available for an immediate consultation. I regarded the patients waiting for X-ray treatments with the same compassion as for auto accident victims. I had surgery scars like skid marks from my collision with disease.

I complained of a continual dry mouth. I didn't have the saliva to chew sticks of gum. Dr. Anderson explained that the sensation of being "cotton-mouthed" was due to permanent radiation damage to my salivary glands. He reminded me of the series of cobalt treatments to the Hodgkin's-infected lymph nodes in my neck. I felt that I was too young to end my double-bubble days, but at least I still had the joke printed inside the wrapper.

When the examination showed no new abnormalities, I asked Dr. Anderson if I could possibly be in a permanent remission.

He answered, "We'll wait and see."

I thought he could have done better by saying, "Let's hope so." *A patient is always examining a doctor's bedside manner, sometimes with the same intensity that he is looking for disease.*

July 10

Replacing the receiver, I thought the telephone message had been exactly like the first paragraph of a news story. A reporter from the *New York Times* was coming to our house. I knew How Who was coming Where and Why.

I impressed upon the children that this was a serious situation. I took the evening paper to the dinner table and read them the possible news: FAMILY AT IT AGAIN

Matthew Lee was struck by a flying pillow when yelling at his two sisters in their Oregon home.	*A Portand, Oregon, family continued its search through most of the night for the missing white flannel blanket belonging to Mary Elisabeth Lee.*

I organized Journalist Fire Drills, which began by my imitation of the doorbell and a pantomime of my bringing in the reporter. I explained that in life we were going to give an account for every idle word. By our words, we will be justified or condemned.

On the appointed morning, a woman called from the airport and took a taxi to our house. The children were playing in the yard. The reporter had perfect hair. Her whole head had made a commitment and was living in submission to her comb. In contrast, my strands were rebellious, doing their own thing and going their own direction.

We sat in the living room to talk. Anna interrupted us in the joy of her accomplishment. She had mastered the two-wheeled bicycle. The journalist resumed the interview. We wanted to take ideas, fold them into paper airplanes, and fly them at each other.

Outside, Anna was doing some problem solving. She decided to lock Mary Elisabeth in the car so as to leave her in safety while she rode her bike farther down the sidewalk.

An unremitting blare of a horn stopped my conversation with the journalist. Mary Elisabeth was securely locked inside, and my keys were missing from the kitchen pegboard. When I couldn't get her out, she began to laugh and jump, still maintaining the same pressure on the horn.

I could hardly say good-bye, I was so frantic in my search for the keys.

Every day I thought of climbing one of the mountains in my life. The summit was my acquisition of a driver's license. I went back to the suburban office wearing my hiking boots and carrying my identification in a knapsack. Securing my appointment time, I planned to practice driving the examination route, so I wouldn't fall into the crevice of one-way streets again.

The official shook her head at the two recorded failures on my learning permit.

"You are only allowed three driving tests within ninety days on one permit application."

She was warning me of the avalanche danger in failing. Flanked by two sixteen-year-olds, I waited in the line by the cement block wall.

A driving examiner walked to my window. Knowing he would ask about the car's mechanical equipment, I blurted the question to him instead.

"Please," I asked. "Turn on your signal and brake lights and horn."

When he got into the car, I said, "That was fine. Now let's go out onto the street and make a right turn."

He let me direct myself around the blocks by giving him instructions.

"Turn up here," I said. "I want to check your skill in turning from two-way traffic onto a one-way street."

He began to tell me stories of mishaps from cars assumed to be in drive, but in reverse; mistakes from slamming on the gas instead of the brakes. He was telling me about the bribes some people offer when we returned to the parking lot. He said I had passed the test. I sang the songs of Zion.

Usually the officer calls the names of the new license recipients. They walk to his desk to pick up their credentials. He made an exception in my case; he came up to me and shook my hand.

August 4

Mary Elisabeth learned to talk. She developed a cassette player tongue; she recorded new words and played stored data. She excelled in taping lists of nouns. Encouraged by the family, she counted numbers, colors, and the alphabet. She expanded to enumerating fast-food chains. At bedtime, she copied Anna's prayer list. Mary Elisabeth asked God to bless the family, naming us one by one.

One night, she discovered she had a picture in her mind for every word except "Daddy." In response, I held her closely and said nothing.

I worried that the children's hearts were underlining what was missing, instead of what we had as a unit. I saw it as my job to build a sense of family.

We spent an eight-hour working day in the car. After breakfast, we suffered commuter traffic until we drove beyond the factories and offices. We wandered on country back roads, shifting our direction at the whim of whoever spoke first at intersections.

We purchased portable lunch goods from country stores that sold jerky in glass jars by the cash register. I kept paper plates on the dashboard and Dixie cups in the glove box. We were contained all day in a space having the same intimate dimensions as a dinner table.

We were knitted in the family adventure of getting lost, then finding our way.

August 15

The news that an English publisher had bought *Walking Through the Fire* was first communicated by phone. Agreeing to come to London, I saw myself in the mouth of the fuzzy beast of promotion, being carried to the top of the World Trade Center. Two years ago, my life had been as international as traveling down the gourmet aisle of the grocery store to look at the labels on imported food.

My parents suggested I make plane reservations to bring the girls and Matthew to California. From the San Francisco airport, I could continue overseas.

Our last night at home, I saw that Matthew had drawn an airplane on his stomach in green flow pen.

Nothing is work until one would rather be doing something else.

August 21

The language I knew stopped at the door of the Alitalia flight lounge: the sound was a room full of electric Italian typewriters. Waiting for takeoff, there were only four of us who weren't Italian. I stood in line next to three African women who carried their suitcases on top of their heads through the boarding gate.

I was uneasy during the flight. Everything was first announced in Italian, followed by English subtitles. The accent of the personnel was so thick that I never understood what was being said. I thought about my plans to travel by train from Rome to London: I knew I would have difficulty finding my way. When I could see the red tile roofs from the air, I went over my vocabulary words: "*lasagna, mamma mia, arrivederci.*" I should have spent the flight painting a cane white and writing in a red stripe "*Americana.*" All the other passengers applauded when we landed in Rome, Italy.

The train station swallowed me, a foreign body, in its gullet. I regarded its size, diversity, and activity as a living organism, whose purpose was beyond my comprehension.

I was on the inside and in circulation. I bought my tickets to England.

August 22

A bus took me from the railroad station up into the stone village of Assisi. I decided to celebrate my visit by eating like St. Francis. I would buy nothing in restaurants or stores. I would live on the naked edge of faith.

Walking across Poor Clare Square, the weight of my bag reminded me I needed more stripping to get down to Franciscan simplicity. I hid my satchel behind a bench in a doctor's office in a corner of the square. Life is more than food, a body is more than clothing.

I asked a monk, wearing the coarse brown Franciscan robe, for directions. He added a final instruction of where the best pizza could be bought. After climbing the cobblestone streets, I rested on a hill above the village. I was hungry.

A family came and sat fifty feet away from me. They whistled and beckoned me to join them. They cut two kinds of salami and passed it to me on a crusty white bread. The olives were packed in a bag identical to America's potato chip wrap. Because of the language barrier, our questions to each other remained as birds that would fly up with no means to escape.

I returned to the square of Poor Clare to reclaim my bundle and make my transportation connections. I found the doctor's office securely locked. My inquiries revealed that they worked only until noon and I would have to wait until morning for my bag. It is reported to be the same plaza where Francis and Clare renounced all they owned. I looked at the square with new respect; it had claimed my possessions also.

The local tourist office phoned a private home and arranged for me to stay there. The house had irregular green shutters and its very age made its shape sway and bulge. I was given a key to my room that was older than America.

Toward evening, I began to wander abstractedly through olive groves and by vineyards. Walking some miles, I couldn't get lost because Assisi is set on a hill. I came to a plain stucco church at the edge of a village. In the middle of its interior was a complete rough hut with packed mud floors. I realized that this was the very chapel Francis had restored for worship.

At the door sat five monks speaking in English, and they brought a chair for me. It was one of my life's moments, when I felt completely awake, and all dreaming and drowsiness had ceased.

They knew I was a Protestant girl. I had nothing on top of my head, yet they included me in the full communion of the priest passing me the silver chalice of wine.

We broke tradition, denomination, and culture. Those things were a glass fence that was shattered by a high pitch.

I sat in the French train staging races for the raindrops that blew across my window. I was engulfed by loneliness. Perceptions that needed another's ear to live died within me. Having no one to talk to, the thoughts were laid in a grave. If I mourned, could the right tear beat the left tear down my cheek?

I wanted to spend my one last night in France in a village. I began to prepare to be born. I stood at the door between train cars to evaluate the towns and see if I could be fathered for a night in their facilities. I pushed my suitcase out and leapt into Hazebrouck. I would again be naked and know nothing.

Every hotel was closed and empty-looking. The restaurant people ignored my questions with a shrug.

A lady with an enormous red perambulator motioned me to follow her. She maneuvered two little boys as well as her buggy. She opened the door of a house located along the main street. I stepped into a parlor that had a few tables for people to sit and have a drink. Her husband was waiting for her with a glass of red wine. Strips to catch flies hung glistening between the antique lights.

The proprietor had yellow-gray hair pinned in a bun and held to her head by a fine net. Black hairs protruded from her upper lip. She explained that she had learned English from some soldiers during World War I. She engaged a room for me, explaining it wouldn't be ready until evening. It was the day of the big fair and the town was closed for the festival.

In the center of the town square was an enormous yellow and black hot-air balloon entitled "Jules Verne." It bobbed with force, contesting the sandbags. To the right was a uniformed band in a box, and I shook hands with one of the members. I was introduced to the Mayor of Hazelbrouck.

A reporter broke through the crowd with his movie recording equipment. Three dignitaries, wearing business suits, stepped into the wicker basket and the restraints were cut. The mayor waved his white handkerchief. The band struck up the French national anthem as the balloon rose above the citizens and off into the sky.

Hazebrouck was my Paris.

England, August 28

There was a two-hour line to pass through passport control. A luxury traveler was equal to the man carrying the backpack. We told tourist survival stories. I shared some of mine:

"Once, when I camped in Alaska, the mosquitoes attacked me. The only way I could sleep was to draw the strings of my down bag completely around my face except for a small hole. I inserted the lace cup of my bra through the opening. I fell asleep watching the insects crawl over the floral pattern."

England had signs for the counsel and guidance of its citizens. "Any dog that fouls the footway" would be fined. A church announced: "Marriages solemnized." The underground subway had continual posters giving instructions in the event that an abandoned package or bag containing a bomb were found.

I missed the children. Being absent from them was a pebble in my shoe. It hurt when I walked and ached when I sat. I called them in California, imagining our voices stirring the fish along the transatlantic cable.

A changing season put a cold fist in the glove of the English fog. I had to get warm. In a department store I selected a light wool plaid coat off a rack. It had no buttons, so I secured it by knotting the belt at its waist. I wore it everywhere, cramming my book promotion schedule into its red wooly pocket.

I later learned that I had kept my publicity appointments wearing a teen-age boy's bathrobe. I imagined the parallel mistake in America: someone scampering across Broadway in a pink quilted nylon lovely with rhinestone buttons. I felt a bit crazy and a long way from home.

My urgency to get to Portland was a force that turned the flight into a wagon along the Oregon trail. I was a Pony Express to be with my children. Nothing can match the speed of the heart's intent. I clapped when we landed in Portland.

The children had left their grandparents and were waiting at home under the supervision of a friend. They had arrived that morning.

We had been apart for light-years. Solar systems had been created, given orbit, and waxed cold during our separation.

Matthew opened the door as I lugged my suitcase across the lawn. He complained about a knot that was keeping the bow on his shoe an inch from the leather tongue. Anna greeted me with a tooth that could wiggle. We didn't move the suitcase any farther than the door. I left my traveling clothes in the entry hall for two days. I didn't want to touch them. I was finally off the fast lane.

September 17

My first Sunday back in America, I went to church. The children of the dedicated members could mature into a generation of artists. The parents press their young with blank tablets and flow pens to keep them quiet. Matthew and Anna draw during the sermon; Matthew pens trains, Anna does houses with small stained-glass windows by the roof.

I was stopped in the hall by a man who introduced himself as Martin Conway, a resident from a local hospital. He explained he had been working with cancer patients on oncology rotations. He was depressed by the survival rate statistics of patients on his ward.

I like some people as quickly as instant cereal is thick: just adding water. Other acquaintances need stirring, attention, and heat before reaching the consistency of a buddy. I was about to invite Martin to my house for fellowship when I was interrupted by the pastor's wife: "Will you please excuse Laurel for a minute?" she asked. "Pastor Iverson wants to speak with her."

As I walked away, I thought that I would never see him again. He would be folded back into the congregation of over a thousand members. He had more substance than the packages of ready-made sweetened cereal. On impulse, I shouted back my address, then went to talk to the minister.

On Sunday, my house is the rise and fall of the Roman Empire. It is strong in the morning from Saturday's cleaning campaign, but declines in the children's siege of toys. I walked over the ruins of blocks and train tracks to open the door. It was Dr. Martin Conway from the church hall.

He took the chair by the fireplace, I sat on the couch. He had a mustache and the kind of curly hair of men who submit to a permanent. He pulled volumes down from his mind and read me stories; he told me chapters from his life. His hands, tied to his sentences, animated his every expression. I interrupted his narrative for dinner and later to put the children to bed. The older one is, the more past one has to share.

September 21

The two little girls sat with me in the front window watching the first leaves dropping. A station wagon with a hospital parking lot sticker pulled up to our curb. It was Martin in a Navy surplus coat.

I felt he was shuffling cards in small talk, then he laid down his hand.

"Just how is your health, Laurel?"

"There have been no visible signs of Hodgkin's disease." I quoted Benjamin Franklin: "*God does the healing and the doctor collects the fee.*"

Martin responded with his own perceptional imagery. He saw doctors as firemen, and relapse as a fresh flame from the smoldering division of abnormal cells.

September 27

Mary Elisabeth had a bad cold. It was one of the small bugs of human frailty that landed on her. I used the commercial repellent of a children's aspirin for her congestion and fever.

Her disposition suffered. She cried when cupboard doors were left open and if the folds of her blanket went the wrong way. She created her own Old Testament law of eating exclusively from the dishware embossed with images of Peter Rabbit. She cried at my offense of serving her a scrambled egg on a Raggedy Andy plate. In an attempt to cheer her, Matthew spelled out her name in colored magnetic letters across the refrigerator door.

Mary Elisabeth demanded one special attention from me: she wanted to ride through the house on my hip. Because of my desire for quiet, I accommodated her for an evening. Later, I slept with my fist pressed against the small of my back, as an ache was the price of my mothering.

The next day my patience was in a tug of war with exasperation. I called the family practice clinic and asked the doctor on call to phone in a prescription for a decongestant to the local drugstore. I wanted to ask for the cold medicine that produced the greatest drowsiness.

October 2

I was trying to get to the store. Matthew had a way of squinting his eyes at Anna that made her scream. The baby imitated Anna's loud sound under the credential of being like her older sister.

I was getting jackets out of the hall closet, wishing they were designed with lapels that buttoned up to the eyebrows. I answered the doorbell, and planned to first make an exaggerated squint and then scream at whoever was on the porch.

Martin Conway stood under the light. He had just finished evening rounds. He offered to take us to the store in his station wagon.

At the market, I started a monologue on shopping. I made a statement that was as much a complaint as fact.

"For seven years I've pushed children in grocery carts."

Martin, reaching forward, directed Matthew to step down from the support bar. He swooped me up and put me in the cart. I leaned against the ten-pound potato sack, smoothing my list to read what remained to be purchased. We maintained straight faces in the presence of the other customers that we encountered in the aisles, but laughed across the parking lot. We were a young thirty-one years.

Martin said good night at the front door, bowing low from his waist. His right hand made an accompanying motion of a modified backstroke in water. The children talked about him while going up the stairs.

"Oh, I like him. I hope he will come over more."

"He's so funny."

I thought Martin was like someone who knew how to transform a sedan into a convertible. By collapsing a roof, there was fresh air in an old drive.

October 3

I advertised for a new girl to help with the house. A twenty-one-year-old farm girl applied. Her glasses slid down her nose and she squeezed blemishes on her cheek as she told me about her work experience. She had been fired from a nursing home when an unannounced state inspector found her, not wearing a hairnet while cutting chicken parts. She said that she had been using some of her wages to supplement the diet of the residents. She added that if she were to move in with us, she would also bring her collections.

I asked Rebecca Dobbs what they were. "Plastic horses whose bridles I made myself. They were once exhibited in my hometown library. I collect games, stuffed animals, posters, and tropical fish." I decided she was a character with character, and hired her.

She moved into the basement and spent most of the night setting up her fish tanks with Matthew. I could hear Matthew shout from the backyard, "When do I turn off the water spigot?"

The next morning I found two tanks stacked upon each other in the bathroom. The top one held giant goldfish and the bottom had more exotic species, including two black Congo knives. My dining room had a tank of angelfish. Water giants, which at times required live food, were in a five-foot tank in the basement.

Every week, when I paid her, she bought either a game, a stuffed animal, or a living thing. She bought three hermit crabs, kept them in a basin on the fish tank in the bathroom, and fed them peanut butter.

Rebecca had a habit of buttoning her coat over her large shoulder bag. This meant that I never knew whether or not I would be shopping with someone looking as though in the last trimester of pregnancy or with an unfortunate hunchback deformity.

The Alley Cat pet store gave Rebecca a real buy. She could purchase goldfish in bulk for only a few pennies apiece. She came home with three hundred goldfish; mostly, she explained, for the purpose of feeding her giant Oscars that lived in the basement tank.

Rebecca lined cardboard boxes with plastic waterproof garbage bags. My basement had several such random dwelling places for the new fish.

Each child put a mayonnaise jar in his room to watch these cold-blooded animals use their gills for breathing. There were two bowls in my kitchen and one on the mantel. I encouraged myself that it was living science, and that Rebecca was a new friend for the children.

Martin was busy at the hospital, but we began to meet at recess from the classes of our lives. I raised children. I stood at the blackboard of manners and morals. He raised patients.

We met at our favorite drugstore on Glisan Street. It had an old soda fountain with high stools, allowing customers to swing their feet. Milkshakes did not come out of a vibrating machine, but were made by hand. "It's from the fifties," I said.

We began to talk of the pending election between

Eisenhower and Stevenson. He mentioned watching Adlai Stevenson on TV last night, smoking his pipe and sharing campaign points.

We stood up and danced the bop, humming "One-eyed, one-horned, flying purple people eater." Martin paused to comb his hair and cautioned me to stay off of his blue suede shoes.

I excused myself when I saw the clock and said, "I have to go. I'm in a Hula-Hoop contest." The bell rang: he had afternoon surgery.

Rebecca went and visited her old friends at Twin Pines retirement home. One lady gave her a blue parakeet and she put Kiki in a cage on top of our refrigerator. Often Rebecca walked around the house with the bird riding beneath her sweater. It was disconcerting to guests when her chest would twitch and move about. I had to talk to her about it.

November 8

Martin and I walked into a short-stop restaurant for tea. He explained that he had been accepted to participate in a six-week seminar in Mexico. He had planned on doing some of his training in an underdeveloped country. He added that he wanted eventually to live a year meeting the medical needs of a rural foreign culture. His fingernails, against the coffee cup, were trimmed and without grime beneath the nails.

We turned our conversation from fact to fancy. Dr. Conway now said he designed vacuum cleaners for a living and needed a motto for his machine. I suggested he inscribe his canisters and bags with the slogan "Inner Space for Outer Waste." We said good-bye, and knew that we would see each other when he returned from his studies.

I finally folded back the October page of the wall calendar. It was issued by an insurance company for homes in the thirties, but enough time had elapsed to make its dates valid again. I saw one inscription: my notation of a checkup at the radiation department.

I had made the fall appointment last summer after returning from the promotion tour that had included Minneapolis. I remembered seeing that city's streets lined with elm trees, and the number that had been painted with red rings. The trunks encircled were dying of Dutch elm disease and had to be removed. Having identified with every injured thing, I wanted to hear again that I had a solid bark.

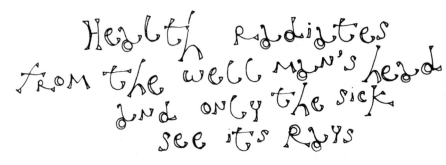

November 20

The first winter snowfall erased every boundary between yards and street. The children took a carrot and walnuts outside to accentuate the face of their snowman. By the end of the day, I could determine the age of the residents on the block by the number of imprints in their yard. Only couples without children still had a trackless white expanse.

November 28

Mary Elisabeth was disappointed with the patients' lounge in the radiation department. She kept repeating that there were no toys. She had begun to associate a visit to the doctor with the family practice office, which kept a box of plastic playthings in the waiting room.

Once in my examination gown, I complained to Dr. Anderson of a backache. I had spent my summer's life carrying suitcases, and every day I had lifted the giant pork chop of Mary Elisabeth.

"You see, Dr. Anderson, I should not have tried to move the piano upstairs by myself."

A wall bracket held the forms requesting the multi-discipline services of the hospital. Between serology and hematology were the coupons for X rays. Dr. Anderson wrote the orders for a routine chest and spine X ray. He said he would call me if any abnormal results were reported.

While I was talking with Dr. Anderson, Mary Elisabeth had spent the time standing at the sink on a chair in the examining room. She had covered a paper towel with soap and was scrubbing the porcelain. Her sleeves were wet.

November 29

I had bought a cotton fitted sheet colored with the marbling of an antique book endpaper. I was fitting the elastic corner over the mattress when the phone rang.

It was Dr. Anderson. He said he had been reviewing the X rays.

"There is damage on the cortical border of the fourth lumbar vertebra, resulting from either a tumor or a back injury."

He scheduled me for a battery of tests, and added, "I'll see you in my office."

Fear can feel like a scale played upon a xylophone between my lungs and the bottom of my stomach. I looked out the window as my thoughts shrieked: *We are like snow. We share common properties but each with an individual imprint. Our bodies melt.*

That night I was unable to sleep, so I sat at my desk. I vacillated between the hope of back trauma and the fear of a recurrence of Hodgkin's. I felt I was in that ancient arena with the two doors; either the lady or the tiger was going to emerge.

Exhausted by speculation, I climbed into bed. Anna had left one of her stuffed animals under the covers. I pulled out her two-foot plush tiger and wept.

I awoke in the dark with one thought that blazed for a moment. The only treasure I can take with me when I leave this life is my knowledge of Christ. In times of pain, I draw closer to Him. Therefore, I am richer in trouble. Then the cloud of the circumstance folded over all depth perception.

I knew Ida Hamilton's phone number by heart. While asking if she could watch the children, I reminded myself of a stewardess talking to passengers about a fire in the engine. "It's nothing serious," I kept repeating.

She assured me they were welcome and paused to add, "No matter what, they always have a home with us."

Hospital, December 5

As a fish that swam by the net and knew the hooks and lures of the medical school, I was once again pulled into their stream of multi-disciplined anglers.

Cris Maranze, my third-year resident from the family practice clinic, put on her waders, walked out into my deep water, and admitted me into the hospital. I was assigned to a bed and saluted my older roommate, who was wearing pink sponge curlers.

Depression was a garment that I couldn't take off. I tried to unbutton it all night with prayer.

Hospitals are known for their drama. First, Cris brought me into the *Bone Marrow Play*: a murder in one act. They draw the curtain around the bed and stab you. The results showed no Hodgkin's disease in the bone marrow.

December 6

I was taken to nuclear medicine for a bone scan. I lay on a machine and was introduced to a shuttle that clicked over my body, moving its arm only a fraction of a distance for each crossing. I began to feel a tug, as the sheet was caught on the arm of the machine and was pulling me to the left. This invalidated the study and we had to begin again.

The machine concluded our visit together by clicking back and forth, only inches from my face. I was overwhelmed by the feeling that I had had a conversation with an android.

The nuclear medicine doctor immediately interpreted the data and asked me to step into his office.

"There are lesions in two spinal areas which have a tumor-like appearance. There is also evidence of arthritis."

Then he brought me a copy of *Walking Through the Fire* and asked me to autograph it for him. Having just heard his assessment of an additional arthritic condition, I felt like crinkling up my right hand in a knot and scribbling my signature with obvious difficulty. Instead, I wrote to myself:

Rejoice in Hope
Laurel Lee

I was airborne in my life and now my body was again hijacking my flight. While floating around the world I was shipwrecked on the reef of sickness. I walked alone back to my room and kept banging my head on the debris of my situation. I found depression to be the eclipse of hope.

The evening nurse wrote on my chart: "Patient feeling depressed, children up to visit. Stated 'I feel uncertain about their future.' "

December 7

The morning nurse wrote: "Patient requested privacy."

The size of the family practice rounds resembled a small class on a field trip. Their number was doubled by pending June graduates from medical school who were applying to the resident program. The applicants knew only textbook associations with disease. They had read about all the properties of water and had even wet their feet in clinics. Now they were planning to immerse themselves as lifeguards.

Dr. Cris Maranze and a man who was in the morning aquatic club came to discharge me. She introduced me to a young doctor, Michael Freesmith. He was wearing glasses that showed the sides of his face through the thick lenses. His tie was maroon with a central golden *H* embroidered in silk. I asked him why it was a different initial than his name. I was always looking for the doctors who were patrons of thrift stores. He replied in a tone of voice that made me think I had asked a question he would never tire of answering.

"It stands for Harvard," he said.

Cris then gave me the parting shot:

"Recurrent Hodgkin's disease seems to be the most likely diagnosis. But other neoplastic and infectious etiologies are possible."

I was scheduled to return to the outpatient clinic for a bone biopsy of the fourth lumbar vertebra.

The pathology report of the sample from the suspicious area would be the star witness to determine if it was guilty of Hodgkin's. The punishment for such cell abnormality would be the firing squad of radiation and the hemlock of chemotherapy.

Once home, I kicked the suitcase into the closet. A sense of separation had set in. I felt I had been pulled apart from human society. In my grief, it took an effort to speak. I quoted Job as if I were a modern-day descendent of a whole line of sufferers:

"Man is born unto trouble, as the sparks fly upward."

The children came back from the Hamiltons' house. They brought to my bed cardboard caterpillars whose bodies had been cut from egg cartons. They had inserted pipe cleaners as feelers and drawn eyes under the antennae. They left them on my sheet. I was reminded of the caterpillar's necessary dark cocoon before its flight with magnificent wings.

In a letter to Martin Conway in Mexico, I outlined my recurrence, and documented it with hospital reports and diagnostic plans. We had maintained a line of friendship. I built a wall on that line with words. The circumstance was my mortar; no romantic expectations could scale it.

My situation had a point like a needle. I didn't expect anyone to come through the eye to my side.

The lamp at my desk cast a line of light under the door. Matthew saw it in the hall and came to my room. He had a damp spot above his knees where he had wiped his hands after brushing his teeth.

"Why do you get to go on trips and we always have to stay home?"

Matthew regarded the hospital as the resort of Portland. I wanted to know what was so good about staying at the Medical Center. He enunciated his reply, holding every syllable as if to underline the importance of each observation.

"There's crushed ice and the bed goes up and down."

Normally I would have chased him back to bed, sticking my finger into his ribs, saying, "And there's ne-ee-edles," but this night I was too sober with every question of the world to tease.

"Sometimes, Matthew, there's no answer but enduring hardship as a good soldier."

December 10

I stood in line at the reception desk to stamp my blue clinic card on a form for routine blood work. They had a cardboard stand-up greeting on a glossy photo of a toad. The caption read:

Eat a live frog in the morning and nothing worse can happen to you all day.

I remembered the first sense of dread I had as a child before inoculation of Salk vaccine as a polio pioneer. I had the same apprehension again, thinking about the spine biopsy.

I went over to the X-ray department because the site of the specimen extraction had to be radiographically documented. While I lay down, the staff radiologist with a Portuguese surname called for her picks by name: "Ackerman needle number 13, Gauge needle number 20." I was given such high dosages of valium and morphine that I cried "Olé" as she began her insertion through the right flank.

However, the resulting biopsy was unsatisfactory for microscopic assessment of the lesion. I was therefore rescheduled to meet with Dr. Matador.

December 15

The children saw only the coming of Christmas. I gave them my word that we would cut down our tree from Rebecca's family farm. I can pull a lot of things from their hands, but not my promise.

Needing room for the Christmas tree, Rebecca went to empty the trunk of the car of her new bag of aquarium gravel and aquatic plants. Matthew waited in the kitchen, pretending to chop his sisters with a broom.

As we neared the land, Rebecca became animated with recent memories. She pointed out the Grange meeting hall, explaining how at every meeting the members had to know the entrance password. They usually chose to name a virtue like temperance or kindness, she added. She showed us where she used to catch the school bus and the Dobbses' property line.

An enormous sign was nailed to the fence: "Get the U.S. Out of the United Nations." Next to it was a cardboard sheet that read: "Goats for sale."

Mr. Dobbs stood on the side of the driveway leading to a yellow frame house. He wore denim overalls and pointed to a stand of trees behind a cleared field. Rebecca's mother joined us with an ax. Her boots were topped with an inch of imitation fur. She spoke of the yard as if it were her living room; she vacuumed flower beds and straightened bushes.

I could hardly walk in the woods due to my weakness. I went back to the car, leaving the choosing and the chopping of the tree to the others. I slept all the way back to Portland.

The roots of the fir tree had sucked minerals into its cells from the mulch under the earth. They stimulated an enormous branch growth that needed Matthew to help Rebecca secure it by fishline. I watched their activity from the couch, glad for help in the house.

My body began to suffer in an enormous energy crisis. I got little mileage from the speed law it imposed on me. I began to spend an increasing amount of time in bed. My visual panorama of a day was becoming limited to the patterns on my sheets.

I began to think of myself as lying in Gethsemane bedding, fervently asking for this cup to pass from me, and hardly able to utter, "Not my will, but yours be done."

Matthew and Anna came to me in agreement on an issue of my negligence. Matthew was their spokesman. He had kept his school uniform on as if formal dress was appropriate to match the dignity of their request.

"We own a car now." He opened with logic and not passion. "We have never put on a bumper sticker."

They did not care what it said. I reviewed some of the categories of automobile stickers, explaining, "It's a short way to say something one believes."

There are environmental stickers that make a one-line point: SAVE A TREE, KILL A BEAVER. Political advertisements are banners for a candidate or an issue. There are slogans of cheer. Religious liners exhort: WISE MEN STILL SEEK HIM.

The children were silent. They had not thought of a cause in which to believe. Matthew suggested:

GET WELL, MOM.

Anna objected, saying it was the kind of message that

went on a card. She wanted to have one printed that would read:

PLEASE MARRY OUR MOTHER. I WANT A DAD.

"That's absolutely too long!" I said.
We decided not to get one after all.

December 20

Hazel had some Christmas shopping to do. She offered to drop me off at the hospital on her way to city center. During the ride she made small talk on what she had to cook and buy. I listened to her as if I were at a great distance.

I felt as if enormous blasts of wind were gusting at me. If I lessened my grasp, I'd be swept into their current, and gone. The children were my ring to hold on to the earth.

At the curb, I explained where in the X-ray department she should meet me at the end of the day. I hoped the biopsy would yield the information necessary for me to utilize the medicinal cure in my construction of a wind block.

In order to maintain one opening in my vein for the frequent shots of anesthesia, a heparin lock of anticoagulant was inserted into my right forearm. As the increased valium dose reached 20 mg, I felt as though we were all the guests at a mad tea party. The technicians were Tweedledee and Tweedledum. The doctor was the White Rabbit.

They had me rest in the hall before driving home

with my neighbor. I was aware of a pressure on my arm. I found that they had forgotten to remove the small IV device with its chamber of heparin. It was five o'clock and departments were closing. The radiology staff had already left. I kept trying to ask passing doctors to stop at my stretcher and help me. I knew I looked drugged. I could feel my hair, loose from my braid, drifting across my face.

I saw a balding man coming down the hall with a white coat embroidered "Surgery Department" in red above his breast pocket. I yelled and reached for him. He removed the apparatus, telling me it was a junkie's dream to be released from the hospital with this intact.

Cris Maranze called me to say that the pathology report of the biopsy showed suspicious cells, but more material was needed. It was recommended that I should have a surgically opened biopsy, which would mean a major operation. I agreed to come in the week after Christmas.

I didn't want surgery, which would weaken me further before even starting a debilitating treatment for cure, if necessary.

I thought, it's the job of every sick person to keep fighting for life up until that moment when it is absolutely certain that acceptance of death will enhance one's final days.

December 22

Martin phoned, saying he had come in that afternoon from Mexico. He wanted to drop off a Christmas present at my home. It seemed a chasm from my youth to old age since I had heard his voice.

Anna let him in, and even before Martin had taken his Navy coat off, Anna squeezed her arms around his knee and rode on his foot around the rug. Mary Elisabeth requested a seat on the other shoe. As they demanded that Martin never stop moving his feet, I ached inside because they had never had a relationship with a father. Sometimes the things that are lacking are more than can be numbered. Children are told to eat everything on their plates because there are foreign cultures where the young are always hungry. No instruction is needed to embrace a dad. It's never said: "Love your father because poor children from divorces don't have one in their home at night."

There are many kinds of starvation.

He extracted himself from the girls, claiming broken ankles, and gave me a box. It was a wooden plaque with one sentence burned into its grain:

All things work together for good for those who love God and are called according to His purpose.

After the children had gone to bed, I thought about the quote. The words could be appropriated like Band-Aids and used to seal innumerable wounds.

December 23

Harriet sent three Christmas floral decorations from New York. Anna put one in each room. I had to overcome my sense of detachment so as to feel I was participating in the holiday. My family was esteeming this day above others, and I was seeing every day alike.

My parents drove to our house with presents in a sleigh of a station wagon. I thought they should own a bumper sticker that read: HAVE YOU ASKED US ABOUT OUR GRANDCHILDREN?

The world's merchants would unanimously elect my mother as their reigning queen for her time spent in stores. She would be given a bouquet of paper flowers constructed from department store ads. The banner from her shoulder to her hip would have a design of credit cards.

My parents accepted my changes from tradition. They replaced a large Santa Claus wall hanging from my youth with a ruby-colored birthday cake.

Christmas moved without my moving.

Hospital, December 28

A surgery day was scheduled and I was welcomed into the hospital at the admitting desk. "We have a quiet room for you on the second floor in hospital North." We used the courtesy and language of a hotel desk, but neither a Hilton nor a Ritz have in their service plastic bracelets carrying the name and the birthday of the guests. The metal clip that held it together read "Ident-a-Band."

My father had brought me to the hospital. I asked him to help me move the thin craft of my bed so that I could view the one constellation of pine tree hills. I watched the furrows on his forehead. I read them like headlines: FATHER WORRIES ABOUT DAUGHTER. But all the news that was fit to speak was human-interest stories from the house.

In institutions, some antiques have a good survival rate. There was a solid oak wheelchair with cane seating outside my door.

A Japanese man came and announced himself as the anesthesiologist for the following morning's eight o'clock surgery. He explained to me that the urology team would move the kidneys and the ureter to expose the anterior surface of the spinal column for the orthopedics. A hematologist would perform the biopsy. Then he told me, in a layer of paragraphs, what to expect from the anesthesia.

It seemed as though he had spent his life going from hospital door to hospital door selling Fuller brush bags full of sleeping gas.

I had resigned myself to an evening's solitude until Martin Conway leaned against the doorway and invited me for a walk.

"It's lovely in the hall tonight," he said.

No one had put back the magazines or turned off the canned music in the X-ray department. He bowed low and asked me for a dance. We swooped around plastic couches, commenting on the size of the orchestra and the ornate dress of the other guests. He held my hand while I made small mincing steps across a bench, using a *Modern Maturity* magazine cover for a fan.

An elderly nurse stopped in the hall to stare at us.

We walked by her back to my room. I looked her in the
eye and said:

*"My IV
did this
to me."*

Surgery Day, December 29

The preparation is the stripping of all identity. My earrings
were removed, my hair was put in a green cap. Even the
two back ties of my gown were let loose.

The surgery department has its own wagon and delivery nurse for patients. Through the sedative I sang the
line from an old folk tune: "And how many seas must
the white dove sail before she sleeps in the sand."

The Fuller brush anesthesiologist met me and talked
about one of his oxygen products. The urology team was
asking where the orthopedic surgeons were. I slept.

I was stuffed back into the wrong body. Nothing fit
and it was laced so tight that I had pain everywhere.

I was born, I slept, and, upon waking, cried until comforted. My nurses spent the night giving me morphine and changing my catheter bag. I could not turn over. So passed my infancy.

December 30

I was aged beyond the nurses' knowledge. They made me sit up and then pulled me to my feet. I shuffled along, leaning on a supporting bar.

Fever and narcotics make dreams. I dreamt that I was bent under the window near my hospital bed, deftly removing loose plaster and old studs. I used the plastic wastepaper basket to hold the debris from the wall. In my fervor, the floor was littered with grit. I utilized more of the standard bedside containers for my demolition. I filled the bedpan with crumbling timbers. I kicked out the last layer of the hospital wall; nothing but cold night air rushed in.

Martin came early every evening, bringing a stack of medical journals to read while I slept.

I waited for the pathology report. A staff member had cautioned me that, even with an open biopsy, there was a possibility of again not obtaining a sufficient sample from the spinal lesion. A radiologist suggested it might be another kind of lymphomatous cancer. I still clenched my hands around a small hope that there was just an infection.

When at the end of the rope, there is still enough strand to tie a knot and hang on.

I was walking slowly down the hall using my geriatric two-step when the hematologist, Dr. Klein, approached me from the floor desk.

"I have an answer for you," he said.

We walked back to my room in silence. I sat on the bed and he faced me in a chair.

"The envelope, gentlemen," I said.

"It's nodular-sclerosing Hodgkin's disease."

It was now a documented relapse after eighteen months of being disease-free. He began to explain in a quiet order the chemicals to be used in my treatment therapy. He abbreviated all the drug names to one word: "MOPP."

It was a relief to know my certain enemy and method of combat. I was trying to sit up and listen. The room's first warmth seemed to become unbearably hot. I fell over on the bed. "I'm not used to sitting up so long, Dr. Klein."

Once alone, I imagined a drawn sword swinging in an arc above my head. It had two edges, and the writing on each blade was from the Prophets. There was written on one side: "By his stripes we are healed." On the other side the Psalmist wrote: "Precious in the sight of the Lord is the death of His saints." I didn't know which edge was for me.

December 31

I was in the orthopedic wing, which had many elderly residents in wheelchairs and traction contraptions. New Year's Eve found few late visitors in hospital North. I walked along the floor once and named it Golden Glow Old Age Home. It was a unanimous in-room celebration of television watching. Each room chose Lawrence Welk's Big Band, and for three hours New York would be one year ahead of Oregon.

I went to sleep at eleven-thirty pretending that at Golden Glow Home I had one prize picture of myself and Bing Crosby that was signed and dated.

January 1, 1978

My parents and Mary Elisabeth visited me in the hospital before their drive to California. My convalescence from surgery coupled with pending chemotherapy wouldn't give me the strength to bounce small children.

Two years ago, Mary Elisabeth had been born upstairs in the same hospital. Because of the Hodgkin's disease, she had lived with my parents from the age of five weeks to seven months. She ate the Jell-O off my lunch tray and played with the buttons that moved the head and the feet of my bed. I had to make my mind climb stairs. Mount one, how long she would be gone, to stair two, it's best for her.

When I said "kiss" she ran to me, popped her lips, and almost touched my skin. There are aches that all the pain-killers in the world won't touch.

January 2

Outside was a winter grab. It rained and froze until a sheet of ice covered the city world. I could only see the frozen trees and hear the weather language from the nurses. There were absentees all through the hospital's staff.

January 3

I told Martin over the phone that I was to begin the chemotherapy. He chanted three times, "Kill Reed-Sternberg!" He named the particular cell type distinguishing Hodgkin's disease.

I waited for chemotherapy all day. The weather was still stranding staff members at home.

In the early evening, a bearded doctor with a name badge that read Dr. Goodnight began to tell me again about some of the MOPP chemicals. "The nitrogen mustard will probably nauseate you and the vincristine could cause hair loss."

The IV's were later brought in. I was given an anti-nausea shot and a sedative. I slept and awoke to vomit.

I was so sick that I lived on top of a towel and a special basin. No one could tell me how long the effects would last.

In my mind, I begged to be taken off all the machines that were keeping me alive so I could die. But I wasn't attached to a single visible tool.

I passed my jagged little season. Even the moon came up that night.

"Oh, time bomb body, I can hardly see your fuse."

January 4

The diagnostic plan for me also included daily radiation treatments to be administered on an outpatient basis.

Radiation departments have to be by law in the basements of institutions, providing additional insulation of their rays from the world.

One transportation orderly was an Indian. From the elevator door were three black signs with white underlining arrows pointing in the direction of the treatment area. As he pushed me past the signs mounted every twenty feet, I thought we had never done away with the arrows of warfare, but had civilized them. I am captive again to the ceremonial fire of modern technology.

The corridor led past the occupational therapy lounge. I had a brief glimpse of looms and one small boy stringing beads.

January 5

The doctors from the morning rounds left orders for me to be discharged from the hospital. I expected to feel better once I emerged into the nonhospital world, as if the disease only lay along the corridors and wasn't out in the streets.

Martin gave me a call, and I shared with him the news of my morning release. He asked to take me home. He could borrow time to transport me by missing lunch and a lecture on pediatric heart murmurs.

I sat in the hall waiting for the final sack of prescriptions. I was weak from the excavations that had exhausted my natural resources. By contrast, Martin was pacing up and down, extravagant with energy. The lines on his face tightened from tension. He told the nurse who brought the pills that he was about to call the pharmacist. I saw that Martin had a potential for irritation that could equal his humor.

I left Martin talking with Rebecca to go up to my room. Matthew and Anna would be at the Hamiltons' house during my convalescence. I was still a door upon hinges, turning every which way upon my bed.

In the quiet of the house, I dreamt of driving home again. This time, I was alone. I turned the corner onto Seventy-sixth Street to find all my furniture out on the pavement. There was a handmade sign attached to a pressed-back chair reading: "Free for Anyone Who Wants This." I looked closer at a correction in the print. A slash had been made across the word *Wants*, and the word *Needs* was superimposed.

Dr. Conway scheduled my house as the last room he would visit during his evening rounds. Sometimes we were the 8 P.M. radio show on the couch. Rebecca would sit and listen. He called me Ruby and I called him Stan. We dialogued: I waited on tables, while he fried at the grill. He jumped up to dust invisible bowling trophies won by the cafe team.

One evening, Martin asked if I had a picture of my

ex-husband. I got the photo album from the shelf, turning pages of snapshots of growing children to the only family picture. I sat next to Richard, pregnant, with two small children on our laps. It was taken in the grocery store for eighty-eight cents, with a pull-down background of autumn leaves. Martin shut the book.

"I resent the fact that the children's father was like a tire that pulled loose during the drive, and another has to be fitted on and adjusted to such a load."

Martin was wearing a thick shirt from a recreation equipment store. His face was flushed as if his cheeks were reflecting the red flannel.

In response, I had no words. I couldn't explain or apologize: only understand in silence. My throat was so dry I couldn't move my tongue across the roof of my mouth.

January 16

I went to the radiation department, where they calculated the exact site of the lesion of my fourth lumbar. Dr. Anderson called the infected portion "L-4," which sounded to me like a small planet invaded by a colonization from the Death Star. Every day I was scheduled to go and lie inches from Flash Gordon's gun of X rays.

January 17

I dreaded the first day of treatment. I knew the radiation would have other side effects than just destroying the malignant cells. I saw my chart opened on the technician's desk to the page scored for recording the daily rad dosage.

While I was waiting with the other patients for my turn in the treatment room, Dr. Anderson asked a favor of me. He said he had three first-year students in a conference room across the hall. He asked if I would take a few minutes to share my opinion on the management of patients from a patient's point of view.

A clear shock of my own aging was seeing how young first-year students in graduate school seem. The way some policemen look as if their mothers had to pack their lunches before they got into their squad cars. I was brief in my exhortation.

1. *Try to see the patient as a person, not just a disease and unit number in bed.*
2. *Always encourage the patient in a realistic but positive perspective.*
3. *Give the patient understandable and accurate information.*
4. *Encourage patient participation in treatment management decisions.*

One student asked Dr. Anderson about the prognosis of my Hodgkin's disease. In reply, he brought over a skeleton suspended upright against a metal bar. He pointed to the location of the tumor in the spine and said, "If we had a sample of people with this patient's cell-type category and disease spread, only 20 percent of them would still be alive in five years." Someone in the group groaned.

I protested, "It's not true. Any Hodgkin's statistic for a sample has to be dated. One can't make a knowledgeable prediction without considering a patient's physical and psychological resources."

The skeleton was standing on their side. I left the

room defeated by their negative image and pronouncement to return to the treatment area.

The technician tattooed a dot on my back as a precise guide for the X-ray therapy. She encircled it with black lines. She drew arrows and dimensions within the boundary to make a photograph for my chart.

I saw the picture. It looked like a contract between my soul and flesh, and I hoped it was not an eviction notice.

The Van de Graaff machine had a green metal tank with five hoses hanging in loops from the ceiling. As I rolled under its girth, I noted a bronze plaque inscribed:

"IN MEMORY OF JOSEPH DONNER: 1894–1929."

He was only thirty-five years old, I thought.

The therapist had hung a sign to my left on the wall. In a cross-stitch script it read: "I finally got it all together, but forgot where I put it."

I rode home thinking I could trust neither in their horses nor in their chariots to pull me to health.

I was a mother by telephone. My alternate slogan to "Have you hugged your kid today?" was "Have I dialed my child?" All three had a sense of time that was "immediate-present," making their only news activity I had interrupted with my call.

Matthew and Anna would come home for visits. I wore my concern for them as an elastic band under my bedclothes. It was a constriction across my heart. I felt our time together was being measured out in tablespoons and quarter cups. I missed my half gallon of children a day.

From my bed, I taught them to embroider, explaining the art as coloring with thread. Matthew stitched a house with walls that were broken and a door that was open.

By phone, Martin invited me to meet his parents. He suggested we could take a two-hour drive and join them for lunch at their beach house. I hesitated. My face was pasted on an ancient body. I wanted to fall asleep in the middle of sentences. I moved on feet that were carved from wood. Martin kicked away my pile of excuses.

Mr. Conway was hitting golf balls into a flat metal spider when we arrived. Like Martin's, his mother's hands lived in the air during her speech. She appeared to be sewing whatever she said. Some words were needlepointed, while the gesture of moving a loom's shuttle accompanied another phrase.

They remembered the boy in their son. He always wanted to be a doctor. He rode his bicycle to Boy Scouts past the hospital. If the lights were on in the surgery room, he watched from a tree limb by the window instead of attending his meetings.

On the way back to Portland, we talked about our friendship. Any relationship is a series of decisions on commitment. I asked him to be careful and pointed to the shore to communicate:

"Most couples wade out together into the deep currents and depths of responsibility. I'm already out in water that is far over my head. I'm afraid of the undertow you could create in proportion to how close you come to the children and me before turning back to the beach."

He had a six-word response.

"I won't lead you on, Laurel."

Martin opened both hands as he spoke.

We stopped to see the Tillamook Pioneer Museum. When the courthouse moved out in 1932, a series of displays was set up on three floors for public exhibit.

After looking at the replica of a pioneer home, I began to read out loud the small printed slips under the objects in the glass cases.

"Our half of an oxen shoe brought in by Henry Linn of Nehalem. He found it while cleaning his yard. Lt. Robert May was killed in Italy. When his clothes were sent home, a package of these hair pins was found in one of his pockets. . . ."

One lamp built out of driftwood had dried lizards stuck to the shade and base. They were chasing small animals constructed with shells and pebbles. The sign listed a number of local people who had owned it. The last one had loaned it for display.

We made a plan to bring in an ax handle that had participated in the clearing of the Northwest somewhere. We remembered an old bottle and hat that had possible historic significance.

As Martin talked to the director of the museum, my stomach convulsed from subduing laughter and I was fighting collapse from our humor at his side.

February 7

Chemotherapy day turned me into a grocery cart and I pushed through the aisles and the check-out stands of the county hospital. I first wheeled into the Osborne lab to give a blood sample. Two pictures were hung by the procedure chair. One was a photograph of a sunset sent by a patient who had inscribed on the mat:

Though man's days are numbered, ageless is his soul.

The other was a print of a cat with big eyes. I was instructed to take the sample to the fourth floor of another building where women in white coats extracted ingredients and listed them in priority for the hematologist.

Both laboratories had a typed sheet of the patients expected in clinic. It was their grocery list of name, disease, and national product number of the chart.

Dr. Grover Bagby came into the examination room, assessing the budget of my white blood cells, platelet count, and hematocrit. Deciding I could tolerate the therapy drugs, he ordered the appropriate dosages.

As the nurse wheeled in the IV stand, my first reaction was a squeaking within myself. I decided to pretend I was receiving liquid bionic implants. I would be the mighty grocery cart able to push the ones lost in the parking lot back into a narrow line for service.

The chemotherapy cycle included pills that I took each night for twelve days total. They produced thrill-ride nausea. I swallowed a miniature "Tilt-a-Whirl" encased in a gelatin capsule.

February 14

At Tuesday's hematology clinic for chemotherapy, I kept designing lapel pins in my mind.

A hot dog a day
brought the doctor
to stay

I chew tobacco:
Pass with caution

Hope is like
Ivory Soap:
It floats

With my third intravenous injection of vincristine, my hair was threatened because the drug affected all fast-growing cells. I treated my strands with a quality of tenderness as toward an endangered species: I have taken tangles out of a unicorn's mane.

I saw in the hospital hall a young man without a hair on his head. I made my way so as to talk to him in our fellowship of chemotherapy.

He was not ill at all, but tried selling me sticks of incense and a magazine on "god consciousness." He was dressed in orange gauze under his coat.

I told him that reincarnation is a great lie, a doctrine of procrastination: putting off until the next life what only can be accomplished in this one.

I was once too poor and young to do anything but laugh at the health insurance ads in the Sunday paper. Now I could never qualify for insurance. The medical bills came in the mail and they were piled on my desk. They requested amounts of money that made me raise my hands and feel I was looking straight into a gun barrel. Even the laboratory fee for examining my blood work alone would have supplied weeks of groceries. The disease, which had once provided me with money from the publication of my journal, swept back to take it all away. *I thought those that gather little have no lack, and those who gather much have none left over.*

My mattress made a right angle with the wall. I lay there and stared at either the sheet or the wallpaper. I dreamt. Invited for a ride, I stepped onto a platform as wide as my feet. Suspended by a single chain, it stretched above, disappearing beyond sight. I grabbed a link as it began to swing upward. The earth went from squares of green color to a ball in space and was gone. There was no end to spheres of newly born and dying stars.

Then the descent was as swift. I was plunged into the springs of the sea and in search of the depth.

February 24

At the clinic, the hematology doctors decided to allow longer periods of rest for my body in between cycles of drug therapy. They were economists judging my stock and bonds from blood chemistry accounts. They had to stabilize the depression of white blood cells.

Matthew and Anna left the Hamiltons' house to come home for extended visits. They became passengers on the ship of my bed. I got up with them as much as I could. I felt stronger.

Sometimes I would come downstairs to find Rebecca's plastic horses arranged across my fireplace mantel. She purchased several models identical in stance and height. She placed them rearing back, suspended on hind legs, in the center of my round oak table. Their hooves almost touched around a pot of chrysanthemums.

February 28

Rebecca moved, taking a position as a helper at a horse ranch near Mount Hood. There she could have animals outside as well as in the house.

The stairs of my house stopped being the ascent of Mount Everest. I didn't have to make camp every five treads, leaning on the rail. My body became integrated with the impulse to move.

March 2

I had had so much blood work done over the past thirteen weeks that, when Cris Maranze sat at my right side to talk to me, I automatically pushed my sleeve up and dropped my arm over her lap.

"I know I'm not seeing things as they are, I'm seeing things as I am."

She told me that I was responding well to treatment. There was evidence to expect remission upon finishing the course of chemical therapy. It would be considered a permanent cure if I was still disease-free in ten years.

I walked out of the clinic and saw signs of spring. Buds were cocoons holding summer's leaves. *I thought some things have to be believed to be seen.*

The children pounded at the door and rushed into the house as water spills over high cascades. There was a roar and a flooding of every room as they came home to stay. We resumed that same dialogue as if there had been no separation. Anna made one comment. She spoke of the benefit of getting so many new plants since I had been sick. She spoke of the illness in the past tense.

Each day Martin had something to share. He moved his arms as if he were conducting a symphony orchestra. He had plans that were music still in theory only. Martin spoke of the possibility of my becoming his wife.

I thought about a second marriage. It could be a great triumph of hope over experience. With words, he pointed to a path in a garden and asked to escort me through flowering shrubs.

I knew this vision at a distance didn't show the insects on the foliage. There would be small bugs that unchecked could spoil the landscape.

March 24

We made a counseling appointment with Pastor Iverson. The minister's desk had a Kleenex box pushed to the side where those seeking counsel were seated.

Martin kept rubbing his mustache with his finger. He said that at times he resented the fact that if we married he would never be a natural father. He knew that I could never bear any more children as a result of the abdominal radiation treatments. We unraveled our emotion. The fiber of affection was tested to see if it contained any synthetic blend.

Pastor Iverson spoke of an overcoming love that can endure, bear, and hope through all things. The quality of that commitment suffers long and is kind, and is not easily provoked. He offered Martin the keys to a cabin where he could go and consider the whole matter again in quiet.

I looked over their heads at a photograph of Pastor Iverson's own family. He had four daughters whose faces were surrounded by curls. A poem like an old jumping rope rhyme came into my mind:

> *If he puts his hand upon his heart*
> *And says that we will never part,*
> *I wonder what he would have said*
> *If he had put his hand upon his head.*

I couldn't eat and only drank water when I brushed my teeth. I went over to Hazel's house. She led me through the kitchen to her laundry room. She wanted to finish hanging some of her husband's shirts before any wrinkles were set in the fabric.

She chuckled at my condensed account of the crossroads.

"Remember, Laurel, whatever happens is right. Either way, you can count on that fact."

Once home, I opened the book of Proverbs. One verse enlarged itself before me:

> *The preparations of the heart in man, and the answer of the tongue, is from the Lord.*

March 26

When I heard the station wagon pull up to the curb, I realized I had been listening for his motor for hours. Martin came into the entrance hall in a faded blue work shirt. His hands didn't move from his side.

He explained, "I could handle three children if there were no life-threatening disease, or I could handle the cancer if there were no children; but not both."

He added that he had tried, and was sorry. He left, not even turning to close the door, and drove away. His words were the sound of a locking and a double bolting of a gate he had once invited me through.

My spirit could sustain my infirmity, but who can bear a wounded spirit? I never owned a bullet-proof vest. Faithful were the wounds of a friend. I walked upstairs feeling I should devastate each of the Pennsylvania Dutch hearts stenciled on the back of the treads with paint.

I told the children that Martin would not be coming over again. I presented it in the form of a simple fact and thought we would all sink together.

Matthew spoke first. "He wasn't the right one, then. Mother, we are a family just as we are."

Anna nodded her head in agreement with her brother. She said, "We won't look for his initials on license plates anymore."

They comforted me with the same solace that they themselves had once received.

April 15

The children and I put in an early garden. We walked out in single file, each to our own row.

I explained to them, *after the winter comes the spring. After night the day returns, and a great calm follows every storm. If any be in Christ, old things pass away.*

Behold, all things become new.

EPILOGUE

July 1979

Since my last journal entry the earth has made another rotation around the sun. The children seem to be walking on tiptoes until I look down at their feet and mark their growth. In successive checkups the doctors can find no evidence of Hodgkin's disease. They pat me on the back as I walk out their door. Once again I am immersed in the cares and wonders of daily life.

> *They that wait upon the Lord shall renew their strength; they shall mount up with wings as eagles; they shall run, and not be weary; and they shall walk, and not faint.*
> (ISAIAH)

Isaiah 40 - 31